Sleeping Beauty

A Pantomime

Simon Brett

A Samuel French Acting Edition

SAMUELFRENCH-LONDON.CO.UK
SAMUELFRENCH.COM

Copyright © 1999 by Simon Brett (book and lyrics)
All Rights Reserved

SLEEPING BEAUTY is fully protected under the copyright laws of the British Commonwealth, including Canada, the United States of America, and all other countries of the Copyright Union. All rights, including professional and amateur stage productions, recitation, lecturing, public reading, motion picture, radio broadcasting, television and the rights of translation into foreign languages are strictly reserved.

ISBN 978-0-573-08110-1

www.samuelfrench-london.co.uk

www.samuelfrench.com

FOR AMATEUR PRODUCTION ENQUIRIES

UNITED KINGDOM AND WORLD EXCLUDING NORTH AMERICA

plays@SamuelFrench-London.co.uk

020 7255 4302/01

Each title is subject to availability from Samuel French, depending upon country of performance.

CAUTION: Professional and amateur producers are hereby warned that *SLEEPING BEAUTY* is subject to a licensing fee. Publication of this play does not imply availability for performance. Both amateurs and professionals considering a production are strongly advised to apply to the appropriate agent before starting rehearsals, advertising, or booking a theatre. A licensing fee must be paid whether the title is presented for charity or gain and whether or not admission is charged.

The professional rights in this play are controlled by Casarotto Ramsay Associates, Waverley House, 7-12 Noel Street, London, W1F 8GQ.

No one shall make any changes in this title for the purpose of production. No part of this book may be reproduced, stored in a retrieval system, or transmitted in any form, by any means, now known or yet to be invented, including mechanical, electronic, photocopying, recording, videotaping, or otherwise, without the prior written permission of the publisher. No one shall upload this title, or part of this title, to any social media websites.

The right of Simon Brett to be identified as author of this work has been asserted by him in accordance with Section 77 of the Copyright, Designs and Patents Act 1988

SLEEPING BEAUTY

First performed at The Theatre, Chipping Norton, on December 5th, 1996, with the following cast:

King Pantalouse	Reginald Epping
Queen Georgette	Karen Mann
Princess Aurora	Philippa Stanton
Nurse Duneaux, the dame	Andrew John
Carabosse, the bad fairy	Maureen Marsh
Salamande, the good fairy	Sian Howard
Marquis de Tarteauxpommes	Stirling Rodger
Prince Florizel	Stephen Fewell
Smut, Cinder, Pages, Sheep, Scullions, Courtiers	Played by local children

Directed by Stirling Rodger
Produced by Tamara Malcolm
Sets by Colin Winslow

Musical Director: Sarah Travis

CHARACTERS

King Pantalouse
Queen Georgette
Princess Aurora
Nurse Duneaux, the dame
Carabosse, the bad fairy
Salamande, the good fairy
Marquis de Tarteauxpommes, the court Major-Domo
Prince Florizel
Smut, Carabosse's acolyte
Cinder, Carabosse's acolyte
Pages, Sheep, Scullions, Courtiers

SYNOPSIS OF SCENES

ACT I

SCENE 1	The throne room at the court
SCENE 2	The newly-planted forest
SCENE 3	The palace garden
SCENE 4	A corridor in the palace
SCENE 5	The secret room in the tower
SCENE 6	A corridor in the palace
SCENE 7	The throne room at the court

ACT II

SCENE 1	The overgrown forest
SCENE 2	The throne room at the court
SCENE 3	The overgrown forest
SCENE 4	The throne room at the court
SCENE 5	The overgrown forest
SCENE 6	Carabosse's den

MUSIC PLOT

Overture

ACT I

1 & 1a	**Fanfare**	Instrumental
2	**Fanfare and Welcome This Glorious Day**	All
3a	**Salamande's Speech**	Salamande
3b	**Carabosse's Speech**	Carabosse
4	**Salamande**	Salamande
5	**Salamande's Exit**	Salamande
6	**A Spindle, or a Needle or a Pin**	King, Queen, Chorus
7	**Shepherdess Song**	Queen, Aurora, Sheep
8	**Salamande**	Salamande
9	**If I Ever End Up With You**	Nurse, Marquis
10	**Risk It**	Nurse, Aurora
11	**Spinning Song**	Carabosse
12a	**Carabosse's Speech**	Carabosse
12b	**The Triumph of Evil**	Carabosse
13	**The Funeral March**	Company
14a & 14b	**Salamande's Speeches**	Salamande
15	**Hundred Years' Time**	Salamande, King, Queen, Nurse, Carabosse

ACT II

16	**Prince Without a Purpose**	Florizel
17	**Steamy Dreams**	Marquis, Florizel
18	**Awakening**	Florizel, Aurora
19	**Get Up To Date**	Company
20	**Carabosse's Speech**	Carabosse
21	**Boring Dance**	Instrumental
22	**Charleston**	Queen, Company
23	**Too Much Time**	Aurora
24	**Carabosse's Speech**	Carabosse
25	**The Power of Good**	Company
26	**Salamande's Speech**	Salamande
27	**If I Ever End Up With You (reprise)**	Marquis, Nurse

28	**Finale**	Company
29	**Curtain Calls**	Company

The music is available on hire from Samuel French Ltd.

Other plays by Simon Brett
published by Samuel French Ltd

Mr Quigley's Revenge
Murder in Play
Silhouette
The Tale of Little Red Riding Hood
(with music by Sarah Travis)

ACT I

Scene 1

No.1 Overture

The throne room of a royal palace

The palace is an eighteenth-century French chateau, a kind of mini-Versailles, lavishly appointed. The King's and Queen's thrones are set US

Two court Pages run on stage, chasing each other. One hides behind the King's throne and the other climbs on to the throne to reach him. The Page hiding behind the King's throne comes round on to the throne. The two Pages square up to each other, giggling

No.1(a)

A fanfare is heard indicating the imminent arrival of the king. The two Pages look round in anticipation

Marquis de Tarteauxpommes, the court Major-Domo, enters. He is an elegant and somewhat affected creature, and he walks in an elaborately stylized manner. He carries a long staff of office, which he pivots on its point as he moves

Marquis Remove yourselves from the royal thrones this instant!

The Pages scamper down from the throne. The Marquis de Tarteauxpommes moves DS. The two Pages form a line behind him, imitating and exaggerating his walk. The Marquis de Tarteauxpommes opens his mouth, as if to address the audience, then turns and catches sight of what the two Pages are up to

Get to your places at once, you insolent mischief-makers.

Giggling, the two Pages take up their positions at ease, either side of the royal thrones

(Addressing the audience) We are gathered here to celebrate the christening of their radiant majesties' infant daughter, the Princess Aurora.

The King and Queen enter ceremoniously and take up their positions in front of their thrones. They are both gorgeously attired. The King is an extremely fussy, anxious and pernickety character. The Queen is rather resentful of the limitations imposed on her by her regal status

There is a pause while King Pantalouse clears his throat, fussily

King Let the ceremony commence!

No. 2

Another fanfare leads the court into song

Welcome This Glorious Day

All Welcome this glorious day
With joy, 'cos we're happy to say
The King and the Queen have a beautiful child
After some years of delay.
Sound out a hip-hip-hooray
And chase all your sadness away
For Princess Aurora, the beautiful child,
Is going to be christen'd today.

Banquets and dancing and lots of wine,
Bubbly and rosé and red.
Ev'ryone cheerful and feeling fine,
Wetting the Princess's head.
All the court and nobility
Share in the christening spread.

Welcome this glorious day
With joy, 'cos we're happy to say
The King and the Queen have a beautiful child
After some years of delay.
Sound out a hip-hip-hooray
And chase all your sadness away
For Princess Aurora, the beautiful child,
Is going to be christen'd today.

The cast form a ceremonial tableau as if this is the end of the song

Act I, Scene 1 3

King (*speaking*) Excellent, excellent! A very dignified christening ceremony.
Queen (*clearing her throat*) Erm — there was one thing, my love, wrong with it.
King Oh, and what was that, my angel?
Queen We didn't have the baby with us.
King What? (*Consternated*) Ah. Marquis de Tarteauxpommes, where is the Princess Aurora?
Marquis Oh. Oh dear, I'm afraid, your majesty, by some inadvertent oversight, I forgot about the baby. What will you think of me?

Nurse Duneaux, the dame, comes bustling on to the stage. She is dressed smartly; but in a manner that shows her social inferiority to the Marquis and the royal family. She carries the baby Princess Aurora, who is robed in an elaborate christening gown, and immediately crosses to the Marquis de Tarteauxpommes

Nurse (*ticking the Marquis off*) We'll think what we always thought — that you're a pompous twit! (*To the audience*) Oh, hallo. I'm Nurse Duneaux, and this, in case you couldn't work it out, is the Princess Aurora. Ah, isn't she lovely? You can tell she's a princess, because she's already practising her royal wees. (*She removes her hand from under the baby's bottom, and looks at it with distaste. Indicating the Marquis de Tarteauxpommes*) And he's the Marquis de Tarteauxpommes, and he thinks he runs everything round this court, though in fact he's about as much use as a trouser-press in a convent. He's got a face like a bag of spanners. He's a total ——

The Marquis de Tarteauxpommes clears his throat, pointedly

(*Responding to the Marquis de Tarteauxpommes; to the audience*) Talk to you later.

Nurse Duneaux moves to stand beside the King and Queen. She holds the baby, Princess Aurora, in a ceremonious pose

King Let the ceremony continue!

          No.2: Welcome This Glorious Day (continued)
All   (*singing*) Sound out a hip-hip-hooray
          And chase all your sadness away
          For Princess Aurora, the beautiful child,
          Is going to be christen'd today.
          Is going to be christen'd today
          Today, hooray!

Marquis (*stepping forward*) Ladies and gentlemen of the court, pray silence for the Princess Aurora's magical and magnificent godmother!

The assembled court members look rather embarrassedly off stage, hoping for someone to enter: nothing happens

King (*in a stage whisper to Queen Georgette*) Now, my angel, we did remember to invite her godmother, didn't we?
Queen I don't know. We didn't do the invitations, did we?
King No, well, Kings and Queens don't do that sort of thing. Marquis de Tarteauxpommes, did you send an invitation to Aurora's godmother?

The Marquis looks nonplussed

Nurse I bet that's another thing he's screwed up. Honestly, I wouldn't trust him to find a grape in a vineyard.
Marquis Now, just a minute, you ill-mannered ——

There is a puff of smoke. Salamande, the good fairy, appears. She is resplendent in a white costume and is waving a wand. She is generous, well-intentioned and always slightly harassed

Salamande	Don't panic! With a flourish of my magic wand, I'm here with you! My name is Salamande! I came along as quickly as I could, But life gets busy when you're representing good.
King	Don't worry. You are welcome to our court.
Salamande	I thank you, sire. And now I think I ought To see the baby you have waited for So long.
Nurse	(*stepping forward with the baby*) She's here.
Salamande	(*looking at the baby*) Already I adore The little mite. To work! (*She waves her wand over the baby*)

No.3(a): Salamande's Speech

(*Singing*) She'll be the happiest child on whom
   fortune's smiled
Since the dawning of the universe.
She'll grow strong and healthy. Are you listening, Nurse?
She'll live in peace and harmony, joy and love.

Act I, Scene 1

There is a sudden puff of smoke from the opposite side of the stage. Carabosse, the evil fairy, appears, attended by two hideous small acolytes, Cinder and Smut. She is old and cruel, magnificently dressed in black and carries a wand

The court recoils in horror at her appearance

The music continues to underscore the dialogue

Carabosse (*speaking*) Peace? Harmony? Joy? Love? I don't think so.
Aurora's life will be all pain and loss
That is the prophecy of Carabosse!

Smut
Cinder } (*joining in with the "s" of Carabosse*) Sssss.

Salamande (*speaking*) We meet again! When evil goes berserk,
I always know it's Carabosse's work!
And now again your evil eye is glistening

Carabosse (*screaming with fury*) Why was I not invited to the christening?
King (*turning to the Marquis in some confusion*) Er, well, we thought …
Queen (*in confusion*) Maybe we just forgot …
Carabosse (*speaking*) You will regret that oversight a lot.
(*She moves and hovers menacingly over Aurora*)
All of Aurora's luck I will reverse!
Her life I'll blight with Carabosse's curse!

Smut
Cinder } (*joining in with the "s" of Carabosse*) Sssss.

Salamande (*speaking*) You are too late. For I've just cast a spell
That will protect her, keep her safe and well,
And fair and fortunate through all her years.

Carabosse (*speaking*) Not many years! Prepare your tears
For when you hear what I will prophesy –
(*She waves her wand, magically over the baby*)
Before she is eighteen, the child will die!

The assembled court gasps in horror

No 3(b): Carabosse's Speech
(*Singing*) She'll prick her finger, I can now reveal,
Upon the spindle of a spinning wheel!
And from that moment she'll breathe no more!
The fairy's spell has got a fatal flaw
Aurora has to die (*to the King and Queen*) but you'll live
    long

In anguish when you think where you went wrong
And ev'ry day you'll feel the pain and loss
And suffer from the curse of Carabosse.

Smut \
Cinder / (*joining in with the last "s" of Carabosse*) Sss!

Carabosse, Smut and Cinder disappear in a puff of smoke

There is consternation in the court

Nurse (*wringing her hands and going over the top*) Oh, no! My lovely little baby Aurora! You horrid old witch, you Carabosse! My poor little Aurora's can't die! I'd rather die myself than let the poor little mite ——
King Nurse, for heaven's sake, shut up!
Queen Yes, put a sock in it!
King (*wincing*) My angel, queens don't use expressions like that.
Queen (*properly subdued*) No, sorry, my love. (*She turns to Salamande*) But, Salamande, can't you undo the spell?
Salamande No. Carabosse has cast it far too well.
Queen (*tearfully*) There's really no escape? Our child must die?
Salamande (*thinking it through*) I'm not so sure. I cannot nullify

No. 4: Salamande

(*Singing*) The witch's curse, so tightly has she bound it
And yet perhaps we'll somehow get around it
For if Aurora lives to be eighteen,
The threat will vanish like it's never been.
King Pantalouse, your hopes can now rekindle
Ensure your daughter never sees ——
(*speaking*) a spindle!
King (*speaking*) But how? In every house there stands a spinning wheel.
Salamande (*speaking*) Not if you ban them.
(*singing*) Forbid them under royal seal to stand
In every single household in the land.
Destroy all spindles! Once organized,
The witch's curse cannot be realized.
Aurora will survive!
All Survive?
King (*speaking*) We'll all be as we were!
Salamande She'll live the blessed life I promised her!

Act I, Scene 1

No. 5: Salamande's Exit
(*Speaking*) Now I must go. Beneath the sun,
There's always evil needs to be undone.
(*She sways, as if pulled by unseen forces*)
The vibes are calling me to Russia and beyond,
But if you ever need me, just call "Come back, Salamande!"

Salamande vanishes in a puff of smoke

There is a hubbub in the court

Nurse (*wringing her hands; over the top*) Do hope it'll work! I do hope it can all be sorted out! I do hope ——
Marquis Silence for ——
Nurse (*continuing unabashed*) I do hope the poor little darling doesn't prick her darling little finger on a ——
Marquis *Silence!!!* ——

Nurse Duneaux is finally silent

—— for his serene and magnanimous majesty, King Pantalouse!
King Yes, and silence for my royal decree!

No.6: A Spindle, or a Needle or a Pin
(*Singing*) I am making this decree to go thro' out my Kingdom
Words that must be list'n'd to and learnt
That all the spinning wheels there are should be impounded,
Then the spindles be destroy'd and burnt.
And anyone who disobeys will be arrested

Queen (*singing*) It's criminal, a felony, a sin —
King (*singing*) And they will have their heads chopp'd off if they possess
A spindle or a needle or a pin.

All Hear his edict, pass the word around.
We all will be arrested if within our house is found
A spindle or a needle or a pin.

King If you wait for eighteen years this law will be rescinded,
Then Aurora's safety will be sure,
And spinning wheels again will cease to be illegal.
Until then you must obey the law.
These measures are the only way to save Aurora.

Queen	(*speaking*) So you must take it on the chin.
King	(*singing*) You risk the greatest penalty if you possess A spindle or a needle or a pin.
All	Hear his edict, pass the word around. We all will be arrested if within our house is found A spindle or a needle or a pin. (*Speaking*) A spindle, a needle or a pin

At the end of the song the cast form a tableau

A cloth depicting a formal forest of young trees, with graceful Grecian columns and a few pieces of garden architecture in amongst the trees, comes across the stage

SCENE 2

In front of the new forest cloth

Nurse Duneaux enters and waves to the audience

Nurse Duneaux (*addressing the audience directly*) Hallo, everyone. All all right, are you? Good. (*She looks round the auditorium*) Theatre's looking lovely, isn't it? I always think things're better when they've been touched up a bit ... (*winking to the audience*) and believe me, I know what I'm talking about. Incidentally, for the benefit of those who might be interested ... (*pointing at a man in the front row*) and I can tell *you're* interested. Oh yes. what's your name, by the way? (*The man in the audience gives his name*) Well, (*man's name*), you'll be extremely glad to hear that I'm single. Single, yes ... but open to offers. Mmm, I'm not so much "On the shelf" as ... what's the expression? (*As if responding to someone in the audience*) Oy! Who said "past your sell-by date"? No, it's just that I never did marry. Well, you see it's now 1785, so I grew up in a generation that believed in "saving it for marriage". As you can imagine, having reached the age that I now have, I've got an awful lot saved up! So if any of you men out there do fancy coming round to my dressing-room after the show... well, just make sure you form an orderly queue behind (*man's name*) — OK? Anyway, doesn't time fly. Oh, it does, it does. I mean, do you remember Princess Aurora's christening? You know, when there was that barney between Carabosse and Salamande? Remember that? Well, how long ago would you say that was? (*Responding to someone from the audience*) Two minutes? Really, madam, I'd take that watch back to the shop if I was you — and complain. That christening happened nearly

Act I, Scene 3

eighteen years ago. Nearly eighteen years. And what that means, of course, is that tomorrow is the Princess Aurora's eighteenth birthday. Yes and you all know the significance of that, don't you? (*Responding to someone from the audience*) What? She can buy herself a drink in a pub? Honestly! Who let this riff-raff in? Last audience we had weren't common like you lot. So, anyway, tomorrow's Aurora's birthday and ... (*She has an idea*) Birthdays. Ooh, birthdays. I haven't talked about the birthdays of the people in the audience yet, have I? Because, d'you know — yes, that's my name, isn't it? D'you know — we have some people here who're celebrating their birthdays this very day. (*She goes into a routine of congratulating those in the audience who have birthdays and leading the rest in singing* Happy Birthday To You) Anyway, as I say, tomorrow we'll all be singing that to the Princess Aurora. She'll be eighteen, and of course that means that the danger from Carabosse's spell will be over. It'll have no power to harm the Princess — and so she'll be able to live happily ever after for the rest of her life. Isn't that wonderful? Right, anyway, I must be off now to join the Queen and Aurora in the palace garden, where they're deeply involved in their latest idiotic game. But, I'll —— (*She lasciviously blows a kiss to the man in the front row*) see you later, (*man's name*). 'Bye, 'Bye!

Nurse Duneaux exits waving

The cloth pulls back to reveal the full stage

Scene 3

The palace garden. It is a formal eighteenth-century garden befitting the kind of chateau in Scene 1

Queen Georgette and the Princess Aurora, both holding fancy crooks, and wearing elaborate shepherdess-style bonnets and aprons, stand in front of four cud-chewing sheep. One sheep is larger than the others

No.7: Shepherdess Song

The Queen sings the following song very seriously. But Aurora is more inclined to send it up. The first verse and chorus is sung straight

Queen I'm a simple shepherdess,
With my simple little shepherd's crook.
In a simple rustic dress!
Simply wonderful I look!

Aurora	I'm a simpler shepherdess, Just a simple little country miss. None would guess my rank's Princess If they should see me dress'd like this.
Queen } *La la (etc.) chorus* **Aurora**	
Queen	I'm a working shepherdess, Simply picking up a buttercup.

During the following lines Aurora's sense of mischief comes to the fore

Aurora	If the sheep should make a mess Your staff will simply mop it up.
Queen	*(with a slight take of resentment towards her daughter)* You will never be a shepherdess, Unless you take a tip or two. Mind your step, pick up your dress.
Aurora	Mother, what's that on your shoe?

The Queen tries to scrape the muck off her shoe, as Aurora turns to the sheep and starts conducting them in the chorus. Queen Georgette is not amused

Sheep	*Ba ba (etc.) chorus*
Queen	I'm a simple shepherdess, And I'm getting closer to the land.
Aurora	But I'm finding ruralness Is more than I can stand.
Queen	I'm a simple shepherdess ——
Aurora	But the sheep all look and sound the same. I am bored and I confess
Queen	Come along and play the game!

The Queen tries to sing her straight laaing chorus, but is vocally swamped by Aurora's version

Aurora	Bored, bored, bored, bored Bored is what we are. Play with sheep? We say...	**Queen**	*La la (etc.) chorus*

Act I, Scene 3   11

Aurora   } Bah!
The Sheep

During the following dialogue, three of the sheep amble off stage, leaving the largest sheep on stage nibbling at greenery

Queen   (*turning on her daughter*) Aurora, you weren't entering into the spirit of the thing at all.
Aurora Well, that's because it's so unreal. Just pretending to be shepherdesses. We don't do any actual shepherdessing work, do we?

Nurse Duneaux enters

Queen   We could try to. (*She turns to Nurse Duneaux*) Nurse Duneaux, am I allowed actually to herd the sheep?
Nurse   Oh no, your majesty. Queens don't do that.
Queen   For heaven's sake! Is there anything queens are allowed to do?
Nurse   Yes, your majesty. Queens're allowed to smile and wave and open things.
Queen   Thanks for nothing.
Aurora I'm not going to be a queen when I grow up. It'd be far too boring.
Queen   I'm afraid you'll have to be a queen, Aurora. That's your destiny.
Aurora But you change your destiny.
Queen   That's what I thought when I was your age. And look at me now — stuck with smiling and waving and opening things.
Nurse   (*looking off-stage*) Oh no. Here comes trouble…

The Marquis de Tarteauxpommes enters

The Marquis proudly pushes his time machine onstage. This is an ornate tent about the size of an old-fashioned telephone box. It is on wheels, and can be entered through the curtains at the front or back. There is no floor, so that when the device is placed over the trapdoor, unseen appearances, disappearances or changes of personnel can be effected. (For stages without a trapdoor, the time machine can have a false panel and be set against a back curtain or entrance.) On one side of the time machine is an elaborate instrument panel, with lots of brass gauges, funnels, spouts, switches and handles. When the Marquis sees that the Queen and Aurora are present, he bows to them elaborately, and then displays his machine to them with great pride

    What on earth is that — a mobile privy?
Marquis (*affronted*) Certainly not!

Queen Then what is it, Marquis?
Marquis This, your majesty, is the greatest and most ingenious invention of the entire eighteenth century. It is a monument to the new dynamic high-potential miracle power — steam. This engine harnesses the contrapulsive energies of the combustible and carboniferous. It ——
Nurse Oh, for heaven's sake! Talk a language we can understand. What is that thing?
Marquis (*with pride*) It is a steam-powered time machine.

During the following dialogue, the Marquis de Tarteauxpommes turns the time machine round, and fiddles with its switches and levers at the back

Aurora Oh, that does sound exciting! I'd love to travel in time. Can I have a go?
Queen No, you cannot, young lady. It's your eighteenth birthday tomorrow. You've got to be here for the celebrations, not living it up in another century.
Aurora (*disappointed*) You are a spoilsport, Mummy.
Marquis (*turning the machine to the front and pulling open the front curtain*) Maybe you'd like to step inside, Nurse Duneaux?
Nurse Well, it might be quite interesting if ... Here, are you trying to get rid of me?

The Marquis moves the machine round to reveal the control panel again, and throws a switch

During the following dialogue, the machine starts to make a hissing noise, and steam starts to puff out of the top

Aurora Oh, come on. Surely we can test the time machine on someone?
Queen I don't know. We can't risk any of us getting lost.
Aurora Well, let's try it out on a sheep.
Nurse That's a good idea. (*To the audience*) Nobody here object to animal testing, do they? (*She doesn't wait for an answer*) Good. (*To the sheep*) Here, you ... (*To the audience*) Oh, that's rather clever, isn't it ? Here, ewe... as in female sheep. (*She laughs disproportionately at the joke, then turns to the Marquis de Tarteauxpommes*) Don't you think that's funny?
Marquis No.
Nurse Don't know why I bothered asking. You know, you don't have to go through life looking as if you've just sucked a lemon. Laughing is allowed.
Marquis It may be allowed, but, for someone in my position, it is very rarely appropriate.
Nurse (*shaking her head in exasperation*) You toffee-nosed git. Never mind.

Act I, Scene 3   13

> (*To the sheep*) Here — you! You want to be the first time-travelling sheep in history? Want to be a space sheep? (*She roars with laughter*) Oh, there's no stopping me today. "Space sheep"... (*She turns back to the sheep*) Well, do you want to be a space sheep?

Sheep Baa!
Nurse Thought you might say that.

Nurse Duneaux grabs hold of the sheep, pushes it into the time machine and closes the curtain

> Right, in you go, my fleecy friend. Over to you, Tartie.

Marquis I implore you not to call me Tartie.
Nurse All right, I won't ... Tartie.

Marquis de Tarteauxpommes fumes silently

> Go on, see if you can make your time machine work.

Marquis Very well. Prepare to be aghast and astounded.

The Marquis starts to fiddle with the controls and the machine's bubbling and hissing noises begin to build up

Aurora Oh, this is exciting!

The Marquis continues to fiddle with the controls, out of sight and behind the machine. Aurora watches, spellbound. The noises of hissing and bubbling increase. The time machine starts to shake from side to side. More steam comes puffing out of various crevices. Finally, there is the sound of an explosion from the back of the machine

> Well, come on, let's see if the sheep's still there.

Aurora pulls open the curtain to reveal that the white sheep that was put into the time machine, is now a much smaller fluorescent pink sheep

Nurse Brilliant, Tartie.

The Marquis winces at the name

> You realize what you've done? You've invented the first steam-powered portable sheep-dip.

Queen And you've shrunk the poor thing.

The Queen ushers the sheep out of the time machine and they both begin to move off stage

(*To the sheep*) Come on, I'd better take you back to your mother.
Nurse (*calling after them*) Yes, she'll be pleased to see you're in the pink. "In the pink" ... (*She roars with laughter*)

The Queen gives the nurse a pained look and then exits with the sheep

Nurse (*still laughing at her own wit*) I'm just too good today. (*To the audience*) Wasted on you lot, you know.
Marquis (*looking at his time machine with some disappointment*) Oh dear. Why didn't it work?
Nurse Actually, you know, I think I might know what's wrong with your time machine.
Marquis I would regard that as extraordinarily unlikely.
Nurse (*taking no notice and going towards the time machine*) You see, I think it's something to do with your transtemporal, contrapunctual sprocket-flanges.
Marquis Absolute nonsense ...

The Marquis and the nurse go out of sight behind the time machine to inspect its mechanism. Aurora chuckles and starts picking up her shepherdess bits and pieces. As she does so, she hums the chorus of The Shepherdess's Song

Salamande, unseen by Aurora or the two behind the time machine, appears quietly onstage, and watches her goddaughter with pride

Salamande (*speaking*) When I look at that child, my heart swells with pride.
Aurora's fairy godmother is satisfied.

Aurora, still not seeing Salamande, exits

And by this time tomorrow, the vile charm
Of Carabosse will have no power to harm
The fair Aurora. Oh, I feel such glee
I'll do a favour to the poor Marquis.
(*She looks at the time machine*)

No. 8: Salamande
(*Singing*) As an invention, this will never fly...
Without some help from someone such as I.
(*She waves her wand over the time machine*)

There is a tinkle of music

Act I, Scene 3   15

>Forget the past, forget what might have been —
>For this is now a ——
>(*Speaking*) *working* time machine!
>(*Singing*) Another good deed done.
>Oh, this is all ——
>(*Speaking*) such fun!

Salamande rushes off stage

The Marquis de Tarteauxpommes and Nurse Duneaux emerge from behind the time machine

Marquis Well, I might have anticipated that your suggestion would be entirely futile.
Nurse (*annoyed*) Listen, you pompous git ——
Marquis Oh, for heaven's sake, woman! You don't know anything about mechanical things!
Nurse Nor do you! You really are a waste of space!

They square up to each other, and start to sing their duet

	No.9: If I Ever End Up With You
Both	If I ever end up with you …
Nurse	I would never try something so hairy.
Marquis	Just to think the thought of it's scary,
	It — gives me the shakes.
Nurse	(*speaking*) My stomach aches.
Both	(*singing*) If I ever end up with you
Marquis	I just never would be so unwary.
Nurse	I can't stand your pride and vanity
	You're so snooty.
Marquis	You would make me lose my sanity,
	You're no beauty.
Both	Doom.
Both	If I ever end up with you.
Nurse	You and I are chalk and cheese and we disagree.
Marquis	Not my cup of tea.
Nurse	Let's keep our distance then.
Marquis	That's all right by me.
Nurse	(*speaking*) Glad that's sorted.

The music continues to underscore the following dialogue

Marquis (*speaking*) Anyway, I haven't got time to listen to your vulgar badinage. (*He draws back the curtain and looks inside the machine*) I must find out what's wrong with this.
Nurse (*sarcastically*) Ooh, do be careful. Don't want you suddenly ending up in another time zone, do we?
Marquis That is a consideration. (*He holds out his keys*) I'd better entrust my keys to you, in case I do get transmogrified.
Nurse (*taking the keys he's proffered to her*) Transmogrified? Don't be ridiculous! That tarted-up tent's not going to transmogrify anything. You're just so hopeless...

The Marquis de Tarteauxpommes steps inside the time machine, and inspects the interior. Nurse Duneaux continues singing the song

No 9: If I Ever End Up With You (continued)
Nurse If I ever end up with you
I am sure that my life would be dreary.
I'm the type who needs someone cheery.
Oh, I wouldn't make
(*Speaking*) Such a mistake.

(*Singing*) If I ever end up with you,
It would be a catastrophe, dearie.
I can't stand your pride and vanity
You're so snooty.

When the Marquis becomes aware of the Nurse's insults, he pops his head back out of the time machine and joins in with the song

Marquis	(*singing*) You would make me lose my sanity, You're no beauty,
Nurse	(*speaking*) You're a case deserving charity!
Marquis	(*speaking*) You're the acme of vulgarity!
Nurse	(*speaking*) You're all posing and pomposity!
Marquis	(*speaking*) You're a quaint old curiosity!
Nurse	(*speaking*) You're a sight to spoil the scenery!
Marquis	(*speaking*) You're coming up for your centenary!

Nurse Duneaux is so incensed by this insult that she pulls the curtain across the front of the time machine

Act I, Scene 4

Both *(singing)* Ooooh! ...
If I ever end up with you.

As the song ends, there is the sound of an explosion from inside the time machine. Smoke puffs out, and the time machine hisses and wobbles about

Nurse *(talking to the closed curtain of the time machine)* I think there must come a moment, Tartie, when you just admit you make lousy inventions. Your steam-powered ice-cream machine produced ice-cream that was boiling hot. And, as for your steam-powered privy — *(she rubs her buttocks a little cautiously)* well, I've still got scorch-marks. *(She goes across to the time machine)* Come on, out you come, you great nit. *(With her back to the machine, she pulls the curtain open, to reveal that the space inside is empty)* Come on. *(She stands, still with her back to the machine, tapping her fingers on her arm; waiting for the Marquis to emerge)* I'm waiting. I'm waiting. I— *(She looks inside the machine for the first time, and sees the Marquis is not there)*. Good heavens. I don't believe it. It worked! Oh dear ... *(She runs to and fro in confusion)* Tartie, where've you gone? You silly old fool, what did you want to go and do that for? *(She wails)* Oooh, I was looking forward to us insulting each other for years and years to come, but now, we're out of time!

Nurse Duneux runs off stage miserably and in confusion

A cloth depicting the palace corridor, which is architecturally in the same style as the throne room of SCENE 1, *comes across the stage*

SCENE 4

In front of the palace corridor cloth

King Pantalouse and Queen Georgette enter. The King carries a golden bag

King *(very flustered)* Now, my angel, I do hope all the arrangements have been made for Aurora's birthday party.
Queen I don't know, do I? I'm never allowed to make any arrangements. As usual, the Marquis de Tarteauxpommes is dealing with everything.
King Good. So it's all in hand. And all I have to do myself is to distribute — *(he pats the bag he is carrying)* the ceremonial sweeties. Must remember, I must throw sweeties out to all my loyal subjects.
Queen *(eagerly)* Can I throw some out?
King No, I'm afraid queens don't do that.

Queen Georgette looks disgruntled

And, actually, you know, my angel, it's something I myself have never done before. (*He looks rather worried by the thought*) Oh, I do have so many responsibilities. I wonder if I'll be able to manage it —— (*He reaches his hand into the bag and produces a handful of sweets*) Do you think I should just practise throwing some out now?
Queen Yes, go for it.

King Pantalouse raises his eyebrow at his wife's choice of expression

King Mm, perhaps I should. (*He draws his hand back, as if about to throw sweets out into the audience*) I don't know, though ... (*He hesitates*) Shall I? Shan't I? (*He pauses for the audience reaction*) I think it's a better idea to wait. Oh yes, it is. (*He pauses for the expected audience reaction of "Oh, no it isn't!" and continues to play on this as long as is appropriate*) No, I won't throw any now. I'll just hope I can manage to do it naturally when the time comes. (*He puts the sweets back in the bag*) Right, so everything's organized for tomorrow. It'll all be fine, so long as nothing happens to the Marquis de Tarteauxpommes. Come along, my angel.

The King and Queen exit

Nurse Duneaux rushes on from the opposite side of the stage. She has the Marquis de Tarteauxpommes' big bunch of keys attached to her waist and is wearing an apron

Nurse Your majesties, I'm afraid that the Marquis de Tarteauxpommes has gone missing!

The King and Queen have already left and do not hear Nurse Duneaux

Oh dear. I'll have to tell them later. Too much to organize now for Princess Aurora's banquet. (*Calling off-stage*) Now, come on, you lot! There's work to be done.

A clattering of crockery and cutlery is heard off stage

Two Pages, carrying trays, enter from the same side as Nurse Duneaux. Each tray has a large, round, wobbly, pink jelly on it. Cautiously, the two Pages cross the stage

(*Looking at the jellies*) Goodness, I haven't seen anything like that since

Act I, Scene 4

I caught a glimpse of the mirror when I got out of the bath this morning. (*Calling off stage*) Come on, you two as well! Those wine jugs need filling!

More clattering is heard off stage

> *Two scullions enter. They are extremely mischievous. One carries a small barrel containing wine; the other carries two silver wine jugs*

Fill them up! Fill them up!

The scullions start filling up the wine jugs from the barrel

Clattering is heard once again

> *The two Pages enter excitedly*

Hurry up, you two! Go and get the bread and the cake!

The two Pages hurry off stage; the opposite side from which they entered

Off stage, clattering and clanging is heard and continues throughout the following dialogue

Meanwhile, on stage the two scullions exchange mischievous looks and advance on Nurse Duneaux from either side, with their filled wine jugs at the ready

> (*To the audience*) You know, I love a banquet, me. Went to one a few months back, and they served this chicken that really tickled my palate. Well, they'd left the feathers on!

The two scullions poise themselves, ready to throw the contents of their wine jugs at Nurse Duneaux

Nurse (*suddenly becoming aware of the scullions*) Why, you little monsters! (*She chases after the two scullions*)

The two scullions scatter, still holding their jugs of wine

> *Nurse Duneaux chases one of them off stage*

There is a loud clattering sound, as if someone's run into a pile of metal dishes

> *Nurse Duneaux, who now holds the wine jug, chases the scullion back onstage. The scullion retreats, nervously away from her*

Right, you're going to get a soaking, you little horror!

The scullion backs further away DS. *Nurse Duneaux advances and poises herself to throw the contents of the jug over the scullion*

And — here it comes!

Just at the moment Nurse Duneaux is about to throw the contents of the jug, the scullion leaps to one side. Nurse Duneaux can't stop herself and throws the contents of the jug over the front row of the audience. The content, however, turns out to be shredded paper or confetti

(*To the audience*) Got you worried there, didn't I?

The two scullions exit either side of the stage

More clanging and clattering is heard

Nurse (*turning round*) Now where did they go?

A Page enters carrying, balanced on his shoulder, a huge french loaf about five feet long. He continues moving across the stage, past Nurse Duneaux

Ah, the bread — good. Now get that through to the banqueting hall straight away.

Just as the Page passes Nurse Duneaux, a scullion pokes his head out of the entrance from which the Page entered

First Scullion (*to the Page*) Oy!

The scullion's call stops the Page. He turns round, swinging his french loaf round, hitting Nurse Duneaux and knocking her to the ground

Nurse You idiot!

Nurse Duneaux picks herself up and dusts herself down. The first Page faces the way he entered. From behind him, the second scullion pokes his head out

Second Scullion (*to the Page*) Oy!

The Page swings round again towards the scullion's call, and knocks Nurse Duneaux over the other way

Act I, Scene 4   21

> *The scullions enter, sniggering*

Nurse You double idiot! Take that bread away!

> *The first Page, with the bread, rushes off the opposite side from which he entered*
>
> *At the same moment, a second Page enters from the other side, carrying a plate with two cream cakes on it*
>
> *Nurse Duneaux moves* DS *to address the audience*

(*To the audience*) As I was saying, I love banquets. Met a very nice man at one recently. Lovely manners he had. He said, "Would you care to join me in a bowl of soup?" I said, "Ooh, I'm not sure there'd be room for both of us!"

> *While Nurse Duneaux is* DS, *behind her the two scullions approach the second Page. One of the scullions points up at the sky. The second Page looks upwards. The two scullions snatch a cream cake each, and hide them behind their backs*
>
> *The second Page looks down at his plate, shakes his head in bewilderment and exits*
>
> *The two scullions creep down on either side of Nurse Duneaux, with the cream cakes at the ready to push them into the sides of her face*

Oops, my shoelace! (*Suddenly, she bobs down to do up her shoelace*)

> *The two scullions launch the two cakes, pushing them straight in each other's faces*

(*Springing away from the scullions*) You don't catch me that easily.

> *The two scullions angrily wipe the cream out of their eyes. They look across the stage to where the second Page exited*
>
> *The second Page enters carrying a huge cake on a tray. The cake is so high he can't see over it, and its top is decorated with whipped cream. He moves cautiously across the stage*

Now you be careful with that!

The two scullions gleefully take up positions, either side of Nurse Duneaux, in the path of the second Page. The one nearest to the Page stretches out a leg to trip him up

Something in the way! Go round it!

The second Page comes DS *in a little detour to avoid the outstretched leg. He then resumes his course across the stage*

You didn't get him, you see.

The second scullion stretches out his foot to trip up the second Page

Nurse (*who moves directly behind the second Page*) Round again!
Second Page Round? (*He takes the command literally, and turns on his heel to face Nurse Duneaux*)

The second scullion trips the Page from behind. The Page falls forward, and the cream topping of the cake he is carrying goes straight into Nurse Duneaux's face

Nurse You little monsters! I'll get you for this! (*She wipes the cream off her face with her apron*)

The second Page and the two scullions rush off stage, sniggering

Aurora enters from the opposite side

Aurora Goodness, Nursie! Have you been at the cream cakes again?
Nurse No, I haven't. Those horrible little... Oh, it isn't worth explaining. Now come on, young lady. You've got a big day tomorrow. It's time you were in bed.
Aurora Oh, really! I'm not a child. I'm nearly eighteen. Why does everyone try to protect me all the time?
Nurse Well ——
Aurora (*pointing to the bunch of keys at Nurse Duneaux's waist*) And you've got the Marquis de Tarteauxpommes's keys.
Nurse Yes, I know I... but I... well, I...
Aurora Come on. Be daring, Nursie. For once in your life, do something different!
Nurse (*uncertain*) Oh, I don't know...

Act I, Scene 4

No. 10: Risk It

Nurse (*speaking*) You must be so careful,
Never take a chance.
(*Singing*) You should never dare, for
Take a risk and you'll regret it.
Stay put, prim and demure,
Safe and secure.
Don't do it.

Aurora Risk it! Take a chance!
Cast aside tradition,
Throw off inhibition!
Trust to your luck, be courageous
You'll survive!
Be unafraid and outrageous!
Risk it and contrive to come alive!

Nurse (*speaking*) Don't forget your parents
Put you in my charge,
To protect and care and
(*Singing*) See all dangers are pre-empted.
Mind you, have to confess,
Under duress,
I'm tempted.

Aurora Risk it! Take a chance!
Cast aside tradition,
Throw off inhibition!

The Nurse can't resist, and joins in

Nurse	Trust to my luck, be courageous
Aurora	You'll survive!
Nurse	Be unafraid and outrageous!
Aurora	Risk it and contrive
Both	To come alive!
Nurse	Cast care aside!
Both	Life is for the living,
	No more misgiving
	We'll survive,
	To come alive!

At the end of the song, Aurora snatches the keys from her Nurse's waist, and rushes off stage

The music continues under the dialogue

Nurse Oh, this is exciting, isn't it? Actually, you know, deep down I've always been something of a free spirit. Attracted to novelty, drawn to danger, lured towards the forbidden. (*She winks to the man in the front row*) As you'll find out later, (*man's name*). (*She calls off stage*) All right, Aurora — wait for me! (*She reprises the end of the song*) To come alive!

The Nurse hurries off after Aurora

SCENE 5

The secret room in the tower. The room is old, dusty and cobwebbed. It dates from an earlier period than the rest of the chateau

There is little light

Almost unseen at the back of the stage sits Carabosse. She disguised as an old crone and is bent over a spinning wheel. As she spins, she sings in a very ancient voice, the Spinning Song

During her song, the light slowly builds, but only to a point that remains murky and threatening

                    No. 11: Spinning Song
Carabosse   Here at my wheel, I sit all concealed, and spin
                    Turn, pull lamb's wool tight.
                    Make thread twisted thin,
                    Spinning thro' the night.

                    Up in my tower, for hour after hour, I spin
                    Like a spider might.
                    Move hand out and in,
                    Spinning thro' the night.

At the end of the song, there is the sound of a key turning in a heavy lock

  Aurora rushes in, carrying the bunch of keys. She stops, surprised at the sight of the crone

The music continues to underscore the dialogue and fades gradually

Aurora Oh. Goodness. Who are you? What are you doing here?
Carabosse I'm just an old woman sitting here spinning.
Aurora Spinning? What's spinning?
Carabosse Spinning is making thread from wool. Fine thread to make clothes for fine ladies. Fine young ladies like you, perhaps.
Aurora How long have you been spinning here in this tower?
Carabosse Many years, Aurora. Many years.
Aurora You know my name?
Carabosse Oh yes. I always knew that we would meet. How old are you now, Aurora?
Aurora Tomorrow is my eighteenth birthday.
Carabosse (*nodding with satisfaction*) Tomorrow. And you have never seen a spinning wheel before?
Aurora Never.
Carabosse It is a wonderful device. (*She stands up*) Perhaps you would like to have a go at spinning yourself, Aurora?
Aurora (*enthusiastically*) Oh, yes. I always want to try new things.
Carabossse Good. Come here, my pretty one.

Aurora crosses to the spinning wheel

> You sit on my stool. (*She points out the components of the spinning wheel*) See, here is the distaff, round which the coarse wool is wrapped. This is the treadle that turns the wheel. And this ——
Aurora Yes, what is that?
Carabosse This, Aurora, is called the spindle.

A breathless Nurse Duneaux enters

Nurse Goodness gracious, I've never known so many stairs. Aurora, where are... ? (*She sees where Aurora is, and freezes*) Aurora, what are you doing?
Aurora This kind lady is showing me how her spinning wheel works.
Nurse (*almost speechless with panic*) No! No!
Aurora (*unaware of her Nurse's panic and passing her hand over the parts of the spinning wheel as she points them out*) This bit's the distaff. This is the wheel... this is the treadle... and this... (*Her hand hovers over the spindle. She looks to the crone for help*) What did you say this bit was called?
Carabosse (*triumphantly slamming Aurora's hand down on to the point of the spindle*) The spindle!
Nurse No!!!

There is a flash of red light as Aurora's hand is impaled

Aurora rises from the stool and looks with bewilderment at the wounded palm of her hand. She totters DS. *Carabosse cackles with evil laughter*

Aurora (*bewildered and weakening fast*) But why? I don't understand. I don't know what...

Nurse Duneaux rushes forward to catch the tottering Princess in her arms, and maybe to save her. Too late: Aurora sinks to the ground, dead to the world

Nurse No! No! Aurora, my little darling! (*She pats Aurora's face and tries to revive her*) Aurora! Wake up! Wake up! Oh, no! (*She looks intently into the insensible Aurora's face*) Aurora, I can never forgive myself for leaving you alone. Oh, my little darling, what have I done to you? (*With a great effort of will, she regains control and stands up*) I must go and get help. Oh, Aurora. Aurora...

Nurse Duneaux rushes off

Carabosse hobbles forward and looks down at the body of Aurora with satisfaction

Carabosse Dead, my pretty one? Dead? (*She cackles, then suddenly speaks in her own voice*)

No. 12(a): Carabosse's Speech
So, poor Aurora, I just had to wait.
I knew one day that this would be your fate.
And just before your birthday — oh, that's great!
Another day... it would have been too late.
Revenge is mine! I rule the universe!
(*She looks down at the body*)
And you've succumb'd to Carabosse's curse!

The music continues to underscore

Throwing off her old crone rags, Carabosse reveals herself in all her former glory. She steps DS

The cloth depicting the palace corridor comes across the stage

Scene 6

In front of the corridor in the Royal palace cloth

Carabosse enters, gleefully singing her song

No. 12(b):The Triumph of Evil

Carabosse   I have been waiting for eighteen long years,
Planning that prick with the spindle.
See I've repaid them, played on their fears,
But I always had it cover'd,
Always knew I'd have another triumph.

Ev'rything comes to the callous,
If they are cautious and wait.
Morals aren't equal to malice.
Love cannot stand up to hate.

The triumph of evil is
Also the conquest of Salamande.
She has no power in her wand.
She's gone beyond
Mere despair.
Summer now ends.
The dark and dullness descends
There'll be plague and pollution
Thanks to the triumph of evil

Everything nasty is so nice
Earthquakes disasters and headlice
Cruelty's fun and it's so me
I am the greatest you see.

The triumph of evil is
Simply the triumph of Carabosse.
They'll feel the anguish of their loss.
Sleepless, they'll toss
And despair.
My reign's begun,
And clouds will cover the sun.
There'll be darkness descending
Thanks to the triumph of evil.
Thanks to the triumph of evil.
Thanks to the triumph of evil!

Scene 7

Throne room of the Royal palace

Princess Aurora, apparently dead, lies on a golden bier

No.13: The Funeral March

King Pantalouse and Queen Georgette enter followed by Nurse Duneaux and the two Pages. They Aah to the music. They all look heartbroken, wear black mourning sashes, and carry white flowers. The King steps forward and places his flower on the body of his daughter

King Oh, Aurora. You are the most beautiful thing I ever owned. I cannot believe that I will never see you again. (*He steps back, overcome with emotion*)

Queen (*stepping forward and placing her flower on the body of her daughter*) Oh, Aurora. You were so independent. So full of hope. You could have done all the things that I failed to do, all the... (*She steps back, overcome by tears*)

Nurse Duneaux steps forward, and puts her flower on Aurora's body

Nurse (*going straight into emotional overdrive*) Oooooh! My little darling, oh, how I let you down! I was as much use to you as a toothbrush to a newborn baby! I was as much ——

King (*trying to shut her up*) Nurse Duneaux...

Nurse I'm so humiliated! I feel like a dog stuck between four trees — I haven't got a leg to stand on! I feel ——

King (*bellowing to shut her up*) NURSE DUNEAUX!

Nurse Duneaux is silent

There is no point in your blaming yourself; the magic of Carabosse was too powerful. There was nothing anyone could have done.

Queen I don't believe that. There's always something that can be done.

Nurse Yes. Oh, I wish old Tartie was here... he'd have some practical ideas, I'm sure. Funny, I never thought I'd miss that pompous git, but ——

Queen (*as a thought comes to her*) Salamande! We haven't asked Salamande to help yet, have we?

Nurse That's true! (*Turning to the audience*) Come on, you remember what she said we must call, don't you? (*She listens for the expected audience response of "Come back, Salamande!"*) Good. You have been paying attention. All right, everyone in the court — and you lot in the audience — on a count of three... one — two — three!

All cast and audience Come back, Salamande!

Salamande enters in a puff of smoke

Salamande I heard your shout. It worked. There was no failure,
Though I was righting wrongs in far Australia.
(*She sees the body of Aurora*)
Oh no! I see a fatal spindle pricked you.
That wicked Carabosse has somehow tricked you.
Nurse It was my fault.
Salamande We'll not apportion blame.
You had no power at all, my faithful dame,
Against the spells that Carabosse has spun ——
But maybe some of them can be undone.
King You mean Aurora can come back alive?
Salamande It's not that simple. But I can contrive
Another spell — not a complete retrieval,
But something that will mitigate the evil.
(*She waves her magic wand*)

There is a tinkle of music

No. 14(a): Salamande's Speeches
(*Singing*)The trance in which Aurora lies so deep
I can convert from death, and turn —
(*Speaking*) to sleep!

Nurse (*rushing forward to look at Aurora*) Oh, look, she's breathing! Hooray for Salamande!
Salamande Just thank the power of my magic wand.
King (*coming forward to take Aurora's hand and pat it*) Come on, my darling daughter. Aurora, come awake!
Salamande (*speaking*)It's not so easy, King. No, it will take
A special kiss to get the charm undone,
A kiss delivered by a young King's son.
King Well, that's no problem. I know lots of princes. We European royals all know each other, you know. I can rustle up a young prince in no time at all. (*To the court, very heartily*) Come on, let's all take off our mourning sashes.

The court do as they are told

I feel so happy, I must celebrate. (*He looks perplexed*) How shall I do that?
Queen My love, wouldn't this be the perfect moment to distribute the Ceremonial Sweeties to all your loyal subjects?
King Brilliant, my love. (*He picks up the golden sweeties bag and addresses the audience*) Don't you all think that's a good idea?

He takes a handful of sweeties, and pulls his hand back, as if about to throw

Salamande I'm sorry, King, but I must stop you there.
You've not heard all the terms that must be met
Before Aurora wakes. King, I regret,
So powerful was Carabosse's charm,
That your fair daughter still can come to harm.
Unless she sleeps a long time, there'll be tears.
King So how long must she sleep?
Salamande A hundred years.

There is a gasp from the assembled court

King But in a hundred years we'll all be dead.
Salamande By normal laws you would. By mine, instead

No 14(b) Salamande's Speeches
(*Singing*) You'll share your daughter's century of sleep.
When she is woken from her slumbers deep,
You'll all be here, safe and sound.
Meanwhile a forest will grow up around
The palace, and the forest's duty
Will be to keep unharmed
(*Speaking*) This sleeping beauty.
King A hundred years asleep! It's almost impossible to imagine. I mean, how long will a hundred years feel like?
Nurse (*to the audience*) Ooh, about a fifteen-minute interval, I would imagine.
Queen Well, if we are all going to sleep, perhaps we ought to go and change into our nighties ... ?
King I need my royal nightcap.
Nurse I can't sleep without my teddy!
Salamande You will sleep where you stand! Now, come on, are you ready?
King Oh, I do think I should just give out the Ceremonial Sweeties. (*He once again makes as if to throw out a handful of sweets to the audience*)
Salamande No, you must sleep!
King But surely ——
Salamande (*speaking*) No entreaties

Act I, Scene 7

Will change your fate. My promises I'll keep,
If you keep your side. Now — sleep!
(*Salamande waves her magic wand*)

There is a tinkle of music

The entire court freezes in whatever position they happen to be at that moment. Their eyes snap shut. King Pantalouse is caught in the act of throwing the sweeties, though none have actually escaped his grasp. Salamande moves DS *and makes a gesture with her wand to encompass all the court. Then she turns to the audience, and sings her song very softly*

No.15: Hundred Years' Time

(*singing*) If you've worries, you should sleep on them deeply.
(*speaking*) Close your eyes, keep them both tight.
(*singing*) When you're unsure,
Sleep is the cure.
While you are dozy, wrapp'd-up and cosy,
Your future is rosy.
How to deal with misadventure is easy.

King / **Queen** (*on yawning echo*) Easy.
Salamande Go to sleep and, when a century's passed.
Nurse (*speaking*) Ooh, I've not done my Oil of Ulay!
Salamande All your misfortunes won't seem so vast,
Seen in one hundred years' time.

Now Aurora's magic charm may seem harmful.
(*Speaking*) I've just got to get it right.
(*Singing*) Now there's worry and alarm in the air.
(*Speaking*) Have I remembered everything?
(*Singing*) Pray for success.
(*She gets her dress caught in the scenery*)

(*Speaking*) Oh bother this dress!
(*Singing*) She may be woken.
By the same token,
Spells may be broken.
I may win and Carabosse may be beaten
(*Speaking*) No-one likes her, anyway!
(*Singing*) With her evil empire stripped to the ground
(*Speaking*) Whipp'd! Stripp'd! Kick'd!
(*Singing*) We'll have happy endings
For evermore,
After a hundred years' time.

Salamande gets rather carried away and breaks into a dance routine for the final verse. As she does so, the frozen court goes into a kind of sleep-walking swaying motion to the rhythm

> So we've got the King and courtiers sorted.
> (*Speaking*) This could be my lucky break!
> (*Singing*) Don't let's panic at the thought of their fate.
> (*Speaking*) Picture it — my name up in lights!
> (*Singing*) They will be snug
> As a bug in a rug,
> Hidden obscure here, they will endure here,
> Safe and secure here.
> Then you'll see the way I manage my magic
> (*Speaking*) I can't believe it's happening!
> (*Singing*) Which I'm certain will make sure that I win.
> (*Speaking*) Here comes the hard bit!
> (*Singing*) So just you wait for
> My boat to steam in.

The disembodied voice of Carabosse is heard singing a reprise of the Triumph of Evil *underneath Salamande's song*

> After a hundred years' time
> After a hundred years' time
> After a hundred years' time!

Carabosse
> The triumph of evil!
> The triumph of evil!
> The triumph of evil
> Is also the conquest of
>   Salamande!

The court once again freezes at the end. Excited and optimistic, Salamande takes up a pose

Carabosse lets out an evil, triumphant laugh as the curtain falls for the end of Act I

The Curtain *falls*

Entr'acte

ACT II

Scene 1

In front of the cloth depicting a forest thickly overgrown, tangled and impenetrable. However, through the greenery can be seen glimpses of the architectural features that were visible on the Act I *forest cloth. This is the same vista after a century of magic-assisted growth*

Salamande appears in a puff of smoke

Salamande Remember me? That's right — I'm Salamande.
I'm here again. You see — I've kept my bond.
A hundred years has gone by in a leap,
And now we need to wake them from their sleep.
We need a prince for all to turn out well,
And here he is — so welcome, Florizel!
Good-looking lad, I'm sure you all can see,
But not as happy as he ought to be!

Salamande waves her wand and disappears

Florizel enters, carring a map and singing his song. He is a good-looking young man, dressed in the fashions of 1885

Florizel **No.16: Prince Without a Purpose**
I was born in the lap of luxury,
And I've lived a life of ease,
But my life has been monotonous,
So somebody tell me please
What do you do with the monarchy
After a revolution?
Where can I channel my energy?
I wish I had a solution.

I'm a prince without a purpose,
I'm a royal without a role,
And you tend to lose direction
When you haven't got a goal.

> So all I'm really asking
> And I hope I'm getting thro'
> There must be something out there
> For a purposeless prince to do.
> (*He looks ruefully at the audience*)

The music continues under the dialogue

(*Speaking*) That's my problem at the moment. I'm all horse-power and no steering. The trouble is, I've always had people around to do things for me. I mean I've got this valet called Tarteauxpommes, and he won't let me do anything for myself. Do you know, he chooses my clothes for me every day. He even puts the toothpaste on my toothbrush in the morning. And I want to *do* things. But nobody lets me.

> (*Singing*) Now the country has gone republican,
> So I will not be King.
> I could even wed a commoner
> Free as the birds that sing.
> But I'm shackled by my history
> And all that expectation,
> And I'm afraid I'm bound to be
> Doom'd to a lifetime of frustration.

During the following verse, Carabosse enters as an old gypsy woman and watches the prince curiously

Florizel does not see her

> I'm a prince without a purpose,
> I'm a royal without a role,
> And you tend to lose direction
> When you haven't got a goal.
> So all I'm really asking
> And I hope I'm getting thro'
> There must be something out there
> For a purposeless prince to do.

Florizel opens out a map and looks at it. Then, puzzled, he looks at the forest

Carabosse speaks the following dialogue in the voice of the old gypsy woman

Carabosse You look puzzled, young man. Can I help you?

Act II, Scene 1

Florizel Oh, hallo. Well, it's just ... I'm prospecting the area because the railway's going to come right through here, and ... I can't seem to find this forest on the map.
Carabosse That is because it's an enchanted forest.
Florizel An enchanted forest? I'm sorry, lady, but this is 1885. I don't think you'll find many people who believe in enchanted forests these days.
Carabosse Believe me, young man, it is true.

Florizel shakes his head pityingly and starts towards the forest. Carabosse bars his way

I would not go into there if I were you. We gypsies know this part of the world well, and in that forest lies only danger and death.
Florizel Well, thank you for the warning, but I'm going to take the risk. Goodness knows, I could do with some excitement in my life. (*He turns away from Carabosse towards the forest*)

Carabosse pulls a long dagger out of her clothes and approaches behind Florizel. This should prompt the usual audience response of "She's behind you". Florizel suddenly turns back to face Carabosse. Just in time, Carabosse hides the dagger behind her back

Incidentally, how long has this so-called "enchanted forest" been here?
Carabosse A hundred years. And in all that time no-one has gone in there.
Florizel (*turning his back on Carabosse and going towards the forest*) Oh well, time it had a visitor then. (*He starts towards the forest*)

Carabosse makes a magic pass at Florizel, who freezes

Carabosse turns and speaks, directly to the audience using her own vioce

Carabosse   Now my cruel knife his jugular will sever
         And fair Aurora's sleep will last for ever!

Carabosse raises the knife for the fatal slash

The Marquis de Tarteauxpommes comes hurrying on from the other side of the stage, just at the moment the dagger descends. He is dressed in the clothes of an 1885 gentleman's gentleman. He brandishes a shooting stick in one hand and in the other hand he carries two lanterns

Marquis Keep away from him, you unmitigated monster!

Carabosse freezes. The Marquis de Tarteauxpommes hurries towards her, and forces her off stage with his shooting stick. Florizel shakes himself out of his trance with some surprise

Marquis Your royal highness, did you perceive what that evil crone was about to do?
Florizel No. And please don't call me "your royal highness", Tarteauxpommes. Honestly, you're so old-fashioned. How old are you, actually, Tarteauxpommes? When were you born?
Marquis You would not believe me if I were to tell you the truthful answer, your royal highness. Let us just say I was born "out of my time".
Florizel Hm. Well, there's something odd about you. I mean, you suddenly appear in my house one day, dressed in the most peculiar clothes, and ——
Marquis Don't let's worry about that. (*He moves across to look off stage, with his shooting stick upraised*) Just make sure that that murdering villainess has gone. Did she say anything to you?
Florizel No. Well, except that the forest was enchanted… and dangerous…
Marquis Oh dear, then perhaps I should not allow you to enter it, your royal highness.

Florizel winces at the title

Your royal parents have entrusted me with your safety and well-being.
Florizel Tarteauxpommes, I'm going in, and nothing's going to stop me. I'm tired of being mollycoddled all the time.
Marquis I'm not sure that I should allow it.
Florizel (*with the knowledge he has the ultimate argument*) Besides, it's in the cause of the railway.
Marquis (*his resolution melting*) Oh… yes…
Florizel This is the age of steam, after all. Isn't it, Tarteauxpommes?
Marquis (*getting carried away*) Yes. Yes, it is.
Florizel We mustn't stand in the way of progress. The railway must be built.
Marquis (*by now very excited*) Oh, yes, yes, yes! How I have longed for this moment to arrive! It is the fulfilment of all my steamy dreams! (*He sings*)

No. 17: Steamy Dreams
Steam, steam — that's the thing that turns me on!
Steam, steam — one whiff and I'm really gone!
Just one little puff of smoky steam,
And — I — really start to have a dream!

Steam — y dreams! Ev'ry single night I find
Dreams of steam. Leave all other dreams behind.

	Steam, steam! Funny, but it always seems.
	Steam — trains rattle thro' my steamy dreams.
	Here it is, that dream again...
	As I lie in my bed,
	Steamy heat — it's driving me insane!
	Ready, steady — steam ahead!
Florizel	Cool down, we've got so much we have to do.
Marquis	Steam, steam — it's just a phase I'm going thro'.
	Join me. We could really get on down!
Florizel	We could steam our way right into town!
Both	Steam — y dreams! Ev'ry single night I find
	Dreams of steam leave all other dreams behind.
	Steam, steam! Funny, but it always seems.
	Steam — trains rattle thro' my steamy dreams.
	Steamy, steamy, steamy, steamy
	Steamy, steamy, steamy, steamy
	Steamy, steamy, steam.

At the end of the song, the Marquis de Tarteauxpommes is quite overcome. Florizel gives him a funny look and makes for the forest

Florizel Well, now that you've let off steam, I think you'd better follow me, Tarteauxpommes.

Each carrying one of the lanterns, they set off into the forest

Spooky music sounds and the forest cloth draws back

Scene 2

The throne room of the Royal palace. It is the same throne room as before, though now everything is covered with dust and cobwebs

There is very little light and only the outlines of the characters can be seen

The entire court are in exactly the same positions in which they were left at the end of Act I, Scene 7. *Their eyes are closed and they too are covered with dust and cobwebs*

Florizel and the Marquis de Tarteauxpommes enter, holding up their lanterns

The lanterns spread a little more illumination across the throne room, and the Lights build as the scene progresses

Florizel Good heavens. Where are we?
Marquis (*amazed*) I recognize this place well. We are in the throne room of King Pantalouse and Queen Georgette.
Florizel Who? But everyone's asleep. And they're all wearing old-fashioned clothes. (*He looks at the Marquis with sudden understanding*) Just like the clothes you were wearing when you first arrived at my house... Tarteauxpommes, are you a time-traveller?
Marquis Well, from time to time.
Florizel I'm beginning to understand. (*He looks at the court*) So how long have this lot all been asleep?
Marquis A hundred years.
Florizel A hundred years!

Florizal looks around the throne room in bewilderment. For the first time, he sees Aurora on her golden bier, conveniently caught in a rather tasteful shaft of light

Good heavens! Who's that girl?
Marquis She is the Princess Aurora.
Florizel (*moving across towards her*) Aurora. I have never seen anything so beautiful. She is breathing so evenly. I am going to kiss her.
Marquis Oh, your majesty, I'm not sure that you should do that.
Florizel Why, Tarteauxpommes? Are you suggesting this is something else you should do for me?
Marquis Well, no, but ——
Florizel I am going to do it. I have to do it. I have never felt so sure of anything in my life.

No. 18: Awakening

Florizel I've waited for one I adore.
I know I'm not mistaken,
For this is just the sacred trust
That I have undertaken.
And so with this, a taste of bliss,
I say to you "Awaken!",
As your lips I kiss.

Florizal bends down to kiss Aurora on the lips. Aurora stirs slowly, stretches, and sings, as if through sleep

Act II, Scene 2   39

Aurora   I do not know what is this glow
                   That thro' my veins comes creeping?
                   I don't know whence has come this sense
                   That sets my heartstrings leaping.

Aurora becomes aware of Florizel for the first time

                   But who are you — the person who
                   Has brought me back from sleeping?
                   Will you tell me true?
Florizel   I am a prince. I've loved you since
                   The moment I first saw you.

Aurora gets off her bier and takes Florizel's hand

Aurora   I feel so sure we've met before,
                   I know I will adore you.
Both   And so always, thro' all my days,
                   I'll live my whole life for you.
                   I'll live it all for you.
                   I'll live it all for you

Aurora and Florizel snap quickly out of this sentimental mood and look at each other with enthusiasm

Aurora I say! I really like the look of you. What's your name?
Florizel Florizel.
Aurora Oh, bad luck. I'm called Aurora, so at least I know what it's like to go through life with a silly name. (*She takes another close look at Florizel, and still very much likes what she sees*) Right, when are we going to get married then?
Florizel As soon as you like.
Marquis (*objecting*) Now just a minute, your royal highness…
Aurora (*seeing him for the first time*) Oh, you've turned up again, have you, Tartie?
Marquis (*wincing*) I beg you not to call me that, your royal highness.
Aurora (*turning with delight back to Florizel*) Ooh, I'm really excited about getting married. It's something I've never done before.
Florizel Nor me.
Marquis Now, please, I don't think you should be hasty.
Florizel (*turning on him*) Listen, I've spent all my life being told what to do.
Aurora So have I.
Florizel And I've had enough of it.

Aurora So have I.
Florizel Aurora and I are going to get married.
Aurora So you can like it or lump it.
Florizel Tartie!
Marquis (*falling back on to the Princess's bier*) Oh. Oh dear.

The young couple go into each other's arms. The Marquis de Tarteauxpommes looks round to find himself face to face with Nurse Duneaux

Marquis Ooh. That's an unpleasant shock.
Aurora (*coming out of their embrace*) Come on, time to wake up the rest of the court. Get kissing, you two.
Florizel (*looking dubiously at the King*) I'm not so sure about that.
Marquis (*looking dubiously at Nurse Duneaux*) And I'm certainly not sure about that.
Florizel Well, you're all right, Tartie. I've a nasty feeling that it's only a prince's kiss that's going to work.
Marquis Thank goodness.
Aurora Get on with it, Florizel. I don't want to marry someone who doesn't get on with things.
Florizel You watch me!

Florizel rushes round the room, kissing all the pages and Queen Georgette. They all come to life, stretch and look around them in some bewilderment. Only Nurse Duneaux and the King remain. Taking his courage in both hands, Florizel kisses Nurse Duneaux. She wakes up, and a blissful smile comes over her face as she looks at Florizel

Nurse Ooh, now that's what I call dreams coming true. I say, young man, you aren't by any chance single, are you?
Florizel (*nonplussed*) Erm...
Aurora (*coming firmly across to take Florizel by the hand*) No, Nursie. He's spoken for.
Nurse Pity. (*Eyeballing the man she's picked out in the audience*) You still here, though, are you, (*man's name*)? That's what I like, the sort of man who'll wait a hundred years for me. (*She mouths*) Still on — dressing-room after the show — OK?

Everyone onstage is looking at King Pantalouse, who is still frozen in his sweet-throwing posture. Aurora looks pointedly at Florizel

Aurora Go on, then.
Florizel Well, I'm not sure I really fancy it.

Act II, Scene 2

Aurora (*quite fiercely*) I said I don't want to marry someone who doesn't get on with things.
Florizel Right! (*He leaps across and gives the King a smacking great kiss on the lips*)
King (*waking up with a start*) Good heavens! What on earth was that? What's happening? (*He looks across at the Marquis de Tarteauxpommes*) Tarteauxpommes, what in the world are you doing in those ridiculous clothes? What's happened?
Queen (*rushing forward to embrace Aurora*) I'll tell you what's happened! Our daughter's alive — and awake! (*Triumphantly*) Yippee!
King I'm sorry, my angel, but I'm afraid Queens don't say "Yippee!"
Queen (*turning to him aggressively*) Well, I've just said "Yippee!"
King (*taken aback*) Yes, yes. So you have.
Queen You have a problem with that?
King Er, no, no. No problem at all. (*He hastily changes the subject*) This calls for a celebration. How shall we celebrate this glorious moment?
Nurse (*stepping forward*) Well, what were you about to do when you fell asleep?
King (*looking at the sweeties in his hand*) I was about to distribute the Celebration Sweeties.
Nurse Exactly.
King So perhaps that's what I should do. Does everyone think that's a good idea?

The King, with help from other cast members, throws sweeties out into the audience. When the King has finished, he sees Florizel for the first time

King Good heavens! You're wearing ridiculous clothes like the Marquis de Tarteauxpommes. Who on earth are you?
Florizel My name is Florizel.
Aurora He's the one who woke me up.
King Really?
Aurora And I'm going to marry him.
King What? I can't allow my daughter, a royal princess, to marry just anyone. (*Looking at Florizel contemptuously*) Now if you were a king's son, it might be a bit different.
Florizel I am a king's son, but since this country's now a republic, it's not something I boast about.
Aurora A republic? Hooray — that means I'm not a princess any more!
Queen And I'm not a queen any more! Yippee! Yippee-eye-ay!!!

Queen Georgette looks at the King to see if he's going to object to her use of the expression again. King Pantalouse is about to, but thinks better of it

King Erm... Aurora my angel, when were you actually thinking of getting married?
Aurora Tomorrow. We're going to have a big dance, and a real mother and father of a blow-out.
Queen Yippee!
King Oh dear. This is most odd. I'm not at all sure what's going on.
Marquis You'll soon catch up, your majesty.
King (*unconvinced*) Will I?
Marquis Oh yes.

The Marquis de Tarteauxpommes leads them into song

No.19: Get Up To Date

Marquis	You once drove by horse and cart
Florizel	Now the railway's state of art.
Marquis	You thought silk knee-breeches dashin'.
Florizel	Trousers now the height of fashion.
Marquis	You thought steam could do no wrong.
Florizel	Then electricity came along
Marquis	You thought a horse could take you far.
Florizel	The latest thing is the motor car!

All (*except Aurora and Nurse Duneaux*) You've got so much on your plate,
You can't stay and vegetate.
The past is gone, the future's great.
What you've got to do is
Get up to date.

Aurora and Nurse Duneaux join in with the end of the chorus

Get up to date! Get up to date!
Up to date!
All you've got to do is get
Up to date!

King	I'm the King. My word is law.
Marquis	No, it's not, not any more.
Florizel	You can cast your crown and care down.
Queen	Great! — then I can let my hair down!
Aurora	Can a princess get some glory?
Florizel	Only if she sells her story.
Nurse	Can nurses let things slide some more?
Marquis	Not in your case, no they'll be on the floor!

Act II, Scene 2   43

Nurse Duneaux makes a face at the Marquis

While the song continues, Marquis de Tarteauxpommes goes off stage. He returns bringing on a large old-fashioned camera on a tripod, with a magnesium flash and a black cover for him to put his head under. He sets this up in front of the rest of the cast

All	You've got so much on your plate,
	You can't stay and vegetate.
	The past is gone, the future's great.
	What you've got to do is
	Get up to date.
	Get up to date! Get up to date!
	Up to date!
	All you've got to do is get
	Up to date!
King	Stop, my love! What does this mean?
Queen	Just that I'm no longer Queen!
Marquis	And you're not King.
King	What, aren't I, Tartie?
	(*speaking*) Great, then ——
	(*singing*) I can join the party.
Florizel	Women's rights will soon be here.
Aurora	Then I'll have my own career.
Nurse	(*with a sexy wave to the man in the audience; speaking*)
	I'll claim my right to a handsome chap.
Marquis	(*speaking*) All stay still while I take a snap!
All	(*singing*) You've got so much on your plate,
	You can't stay and vegetate.
	The past is gone, the future's great.
	All you've got to do is
	Get up to date.
	Get up to date! Get up to date!
	Up to date!
	All you've got to do is get
	Up to date!
	Get up to date! Get up to date!
	Up to date!
	All you've got to do is get
	Up to date!

The chorus ends with the cast holding a pose for the camera

The Marquis' magnesium flashes. The Lights go down and the overgrown forest cloth comes across the stage

Scene 3

In front of the overgrown forest cloth

There is a puff of smoke and Carabosse enters. She is seething with fury

Carabosse Curses! The whole thing's going far too well!
But wait, Aurora and Prince Florizel,
Your celebrations now are premature.
I'll bring a death for which there is no cure.
And when I kill the girl and Florizel,
I will pollute the world around as well.
To make things worse, and spread these evil blights,
I'll summon up my wicked acolytes!
Come, Smut! Come, Cinder! We'll let rip
And turn the world into a refuse tip!

Cinder and Smut come horribly on stage, and fawn at the feet of their mistress

Carabosse sings

No.20: Carabosse's Speech

Carabosse We're going to make the whole earth one big mess!
Are you behind me, monsters? Answer!

Cinder
Smut   } (*hissing unpleasantly*) Yessssss!

Carabosse And will you help me kill the young princess
And handsome Florizel? Come, answer!

Cinder
Smut   } (*hissing unpleasantly*) Yessssss!

Carabosse I'll seize her at their eve-of-wedding dance.
Against my evil they will have no chance.
The game's not over — that I guarantee.
Aurora has not heard the last of me!

Carabosse hurries off stage, followed by her evil acolytes

Act II, Scene 4 45

SCENE 4

The throne room of the Royal Palace. The throne room has been cleared of cobwebs and dust. The Marquis' time machine is in position over the trap door (or by an entrance)

The court, now dressed in nineteenth-century clothes, is assembled for the dance on the eve of Aurora's and Florizel's wedding. The Queen is dressed particularly in an unroyal style. The King, however, still has his crown on

The music begins for the dance

No.21: Boring Dance

During the dance, the betrothed couple partner each other; King Pantalouse and Queen Georgette dance together; and so do the Marquis de Tarteauxpommes and Nurse Duneaux. They dance sedately around the time machine, and they all look bored, particularly the young couple. After a few moments, Aurora and Florizel stop dancing

The music trickles to a halt

Aurora This is really boring, Daddy.
King Well, there's gratitude. I set up this big dance for you ——
Queen But it is boring. The music's so dreary.
Florizel I'm sorry. This is the only kind of dance music there is in 1885.
Aurora Well then, let's not be in 1885.
Queen No, let's not. Is this time machine of yours still working, Tartie?
Marquis It is in perfect working order, your majesty.
Nurse (*to the audience*) It's about the only thing of his that is.
Aurora Great. Then get it started. We can use it to find some dance music we really like.

The Marquis de Tarteauxpommes goes up to switch on the time machine

Queen Exactly. What an intelligent daughter I have.
Nurse Ooh, I'm not sure how good an idea this is ——
King No. Nor am I.
Queen Well, we're not terribly interested in what you think, because we *know* it's a good idea, don't we, Aurora?
Aurora Yes.

The time machine judders and steam starts puffing out of it

Queen (*moving forward to the time machine*) I'm off to find the best dance music in the history of the universe.
Aurora Great. (*She draws the curtain back*)

Queen Georgette goes into the time machine

Queen Right you are, Tartie. Send me on my way!
Nurse (*calling out*) Don't forget the duty free!

The Marquis de Tarteauxpommes pulls the curtain across, and presses a switch. Smoke and bubbling noises come out of the time machine. Nurse Duneaux moves across anxiously to look at it. Aurora and the Marquis de Tarteauxpommes watch it with excitement, leaving an anxious-looking King DS *with Florizel*

King Oh dear, I should have stopped her. Poor Georgette. I feel so responsible for her.
Florizel Why? She can look after herself.
King But no, I am responsible. Kings have to be responsible.
Florizel And do you enjoy being responsible?
King (*having great difficulty articulating the heretical thought*) Well, I... Erm, I... I mean, as a king, one has a duty to ... (*He suddenly takes his crown off*) No, I hate being responsible! I hate being King! I've always hated being King! All I want in life is a job where I have no responsibility at all!
Florizel Then why shouldn't you have one?
King Exactly! Why shouldn't I? (*Ecstatically, he hurls his crown off stage*) I'm free! I'm free!
Nurse (*listening at the curtain of the time machine*) I think I can hear some music.
Aurora She's coming back! Ooh, and the music sounds marvellous!

Very quietly music starts

No. 22: Charleston

The Marquis de Tarteauxpommes opens the curtain of the time machine to reveal Queen Georgette dressed as a flapper, and playing a trumpet. She steps out, and the Marquis closes the curtain behind her

Queen Great! Now this is what I call music! (*She begins doing the steps and singing the words of the Charleston*)

During the song the cast learn the steps and the words

Act II, Scene 4   47

> **No.22: Charleston (continued)**
> Do the Charleston, boys and girls!
> (*Speaking*) Come on, flappers, swing your pearls
> (*Singing*) And melt away your cares in the music!
> (*Speaking*) Boo boo be do
> (*Singing*) Do the Charleston, show your knees!
> (*Speaking*) It's a frightf'ly jolly wheeze
> (*Singing*) For you to dance away till you drop.
> (*Sspeaking*) Whacka doo, whacka doo, whacka doo
> (*Singing*) Just make sure your disposition is sunny.
> Laugh out loud because the music is funny, honey.
> Do the Charleston, you can't lose.
> It's a tonic for the blues.
> It's bound to leave you feeling on top.

The music continues while the cast dances

> *The curtain of the time machine opens to reveal Carabosse!*

The cast do not see Carabosse as they are so preoccupied. Aurora, unaware, remains dancing close to the time machine. Carabosse snatches Aurora, pulls her inside and clasps a hand over her mouth. Carabosse then smiles gleefully. Florizel is the first to notice what's happened

Florizel Oh, no! Look! (*He points to the time machine*)

The assembled court turn to look at the time machine, the dance breaks up and the music peters out

Carabosse Now here's the end to all your celebration.
I take Aurora off to her damnation!
You'll never find us, for when you give chase,
We might be anywhere in time or space!

With an evil laugh, Carabosse pulls the front curtain across. The time machine makes bubbling noises, and steam puffs out of it. For a moment, the assembled characters are too dumbfounded to do anything

Florizel No! Aurora, come back! Don't leave me! (*He rushes forward to the time machine and pulls the curtain open*)

> *Carabosse and Aurora have disapeared. The cubicle is empty*

Florizel turns back to face the others

She's gone! That wicked enchantress has stolen her away! Isn't there some magic we can use to save her?
Nurse Well, we could call Salamande.
Florizel Who's Salamande?
Nurse Well, she's Princess Aurora's godmother. She's ——
Queen No time for explanations. Just call her.
Nurse (*to the audience*) Yes. Now you all remember what we have to call, don't you?

The audience hopefully will respond with "Come back Salamande"

Queen Well, where is she? (*She bawls at the top of her voice*) Come back, Salamande!

Salamande appears in a puff of smoke

Salamande   Sorry that I couldn't get here sooner.
                    I've just been doing some good deads in Poona.
                    But now I ——
Florizel Never mind that! Aurora's been abducted!
Salamande What?
Queen It's true! Carabosse has stolen her away in the time machine!
Florizel Aurora could be anywhere. In any place. At any time of history. Please, Salamande, you must help us find her.
Salamande   I'll do my best, although it will be tough.
                    My magic powers may not be strong enough
                    To counter Carabosse on her home ground.
                    But don't despair. Aurora will be found.
Florizel Do you know where she is?
Salamande   I can't be sure.
                    (*She makes an effort of concentration and looks as if she is receiving a mental image*)
                    I see a dungeon, hateful and obscure…
Florizel   Oh, poor Aurora. I must go and find her.
Salamande   Yes, so you must. And with a magic minder.
                    See, to protect you from the worst of harm,
                    I can equip you with a potent charm.
                    (*She hands a small scroll across to him*)
                    This riddle will instruct you what to do.
Florizel (*opening the scroll*) But can I solve it?
Salamande   That is up to you.
                    Now, quick! No time to waste. You stay here, King and Queen,
                    But all the rest must travel through the time machine!
                    Go, Florizel!

Act II, Scene 4   49

Florizel I'm off—to find my precious love!

Florizel goes through the time machine and disappears off stage

Salamande Next, Nurse Duneaux!
Nurse (*all of a dither*) Oh, I'm not sure...
Salamande (*to the pages*) Give her a shove!

The two pages start to push Nurse Duneaux towards the time machine

Nurse (*to the man in the audience*) Will you wait? I may be ages.
Salamande Just push her through. Go on, just push her, pages!
Nurse (*as she is pushed into the time machine*) Ooh!

Nurse Duneaux and the pages go through the time machine and disappear off stage

Salamande Next, Tarteauxpommes.
Marquis What?
Salamande You. The next one's you.
Marquis Now just a moment. This is not good enough.
Salamande What?
Marquis Your magic. You've sent poor Florizel off with a riddle. A riddle! I mean, he's going to need a bit more than a riddle if he's going to find Aurora.
Salamande (*nonplussed*) Well, I'm not sure... Oh dear, I'm in a flap. (*She has a sudden thought and she produces a magic map from the folds of her costume*)
    I've just remembered. There's this Magic Map.
Marquis I'll take it to him. Show me how it's used.
Salamande Oh, goodness, I feel stupid and confused.

Responding quickly to the exasperated expressions of the Queen and the Marquis de Tarteauxpommes, Salamande holds the map out to show them how it works

	See that small light? Its movements you must trace
	To pinpoint where Aurora is in cosmic time and space.
Marquis	Can't you come with me, to be by our side?
Salamande	Alas, I can't. The map must be your guide.
	For within Carabosse's den her power will be so strong
	That my own magic would not last for long.

Marquis (*making for the time machine*) Right, well I'm off. Although the journey's scary, farewell!

The Marquis goes through the time machine and disappears off stage

Salamande I'm such a hopeless fairy! (*She turns to the King and Queen*) Now we must pray that all will turn out well.
King Yes, it's dreadful. I wish there's something I could do.
Queen Well, of course there's something you can do.
King No, there isn't, my angel. You see, I've given up being responsible for anything.
Queen Have you? Well, I haven't! (*She strides off purposefully*) I'm going to mobilize every person in this country to look for Aurora. That's what I'm going to do—Pantie!
King (*amazed*) Pantie? And you'll be doing this on your own, my love, will you?
Queen (*striding off stage*) Of course!

Queen Georgette exits

King Pantalouse looks very perturbed and hurries off after his wife

Salamande (*to the audience*) Oh dear. I fear we soon may see a royal divorce.

Salamande disappears off stage

The overgrown forest cloth comes across the stage

Scene 5

In front of the overgrown forest cloth

Florizel enters through the auditorium

Florizel Aurora! Aurora!

Nurse Duneaux enters through another entrance

Nurse Aurora! Aurora!

The two pages enters through yet another entrance

Pages Aurora! Aurora!

Act II, Scene 5   51

The cast do a bit of asking individual members of the audience if they've seen Aurora, or if they have any idea of where she might be

Florizel (*sitting down on the edge of the stage*) It's hopeless. She could be anywhere. I don't even know where to start looking.
Nurse (*still in the auditorium*) Well, what about that scroll Salamande gave you? The riddle. What does that say?
Florizel (*reading from the scroll*)
"The power of good the power of bad defeats
When all of these ingredients are blended —
A pure heart, a kiss, what's in the seats,
A stolen song — and evil will be ended!"
(*He looks around at the others*)

I can't make head or tail of it. Anyone else got any ideas?

They all shake their heads gloomily. Florizel muses

What's in the seats?
Nurse Horsehair?
Florizel What?
Nurse Horsehair. It is. That's what they stuff seat cushions with.
Florizel Oh, shut up. We need a miracle to help us. We need a gallant knight to come galloping up on a white horse.

The Marquis de Tarteauxpommes comes hurrying in from another auditorium entrance

Marquis Your royal highness! Your royal highness!
Nurse Oh, well, better than nothing. A pompous old Marquis galloping up on Shanks's pony.
Florizel What is it, Tarteauxpommes?
Marquis (*holding the map out*) Your royal highness, Salamande has given me this magic map to help you find Aurora.
Florizel Oh, wonderful! Why didn't she give it to me?
Marquis She forgot.
Nurse And may I say that's entirely typical. As a fairy, that Salamande — honestly! She'd lose her way trying to get to the top of the Christmas tree.
Florizel Don't worry about that. How does the map work, Tarteauxpommes?
Marquis (*pointing it out*) You see that light?
Florizel Yes?
Marquis You follow that and it will lead you to where Aurora is imprisoned.
Florizel Hooray! We'll find her!

Nurse (*nervously*) But what if Carabosse is there ?
Florizel Then I will fight Carabosse and defeat her!
Nurse (*to the audience*) Ooh, he is brave, isn't he?

Florizal looking at the map, leads the others off through the auditorium as he follows its promptings

Florizel Have no fear, Aurora my love! Carabosse is powerless now! We're on our way to save you!

They all march boldly out through the auditorium

Scene 6

Carabosse's den. This is a noxious sink of nineteenth-century industrial waste. Blackened with smoke, clouded with poisonous vapours, unnamed machines chug and clunk away. At the back is a metal cage, containing an old treadmill. Nearby is the glowing mouth of a fiery furnace, with various red-hot swords inside. Beside, the furnace is a pitchfork. There are one or two broken-down chairs also on the set

Alone in the middle of all this filth, sits Aurora. She sings

No. 23: Too Much Time

Aurora
When I was younger,
Safe with my parents,
I was so happy there.
Time was so silent,
Time glided past me,
I didn't notice and I didn't care.

When I was younger,
I never dream'd that
Life was not here to stay.
Year follow'd year,
I was so thoughtless,
I didn't notice life passing away.

Life was full — now I find
Loneliness seems to
Prey on my mind.
I loved time,
Now I am here with
Too much time

Act II, Scene 6

At the end of the song, Carabosse enters, with Cinder and Smut

Carabosse (*speaking*)Ah-ah, my pretty! Well, you're in a scrape,
A hellish hole from which there's no escape.
You have no hope at all — no one has less.
(*To her acolytes*) Shall we torment her further? Shall we?
Cinder⎫ Yessss!
Smut ⎭
Aurora I'm not afraid of you.
Carabosse You'd better be!
'Cause you'll be here for all eternity.
You'll never see the light of day.
Your beauty will just fade away.
Aurora I will be saved by Florizel.
Carabosse Ha, ha. No chance, for I have put a spell
Around this dungeon to protect the place,
And you will never see another human face.
Just me — and these my minions, fair Princess.
Cinder and Smut, none else … is that right?
Cinder⎫ Yessss!
Smut ⎭
Carabosse And now you must work! (*To her acolytes*)
Come, put her in the cage,
Where she will toil and toil for many an age.

The acolytes hustle Aurora into the cage

Chain her up, Cinder and Smut!

Aurora is chained in position

And let her prison doors be shut!

The cage doors are closed

So, Aurora, now your fate is sealed.
These locks are magic, and they will not yield
To anything — except one magic spell,
Which you can never guess — and I won't tell.
Now start to walk. Come, turn the treadmill round!

Aurora starts to work the treadmill. It makes a mechanical clunking noise

> Oh, how you'll come to hate that dreadful sound.
> And, incidentally, don't think of shirking.
> I've made a spell, which means, if you stop working,
> A thousand unseen needles will appear
> To pierce your flesh.

Aurora stops on the treadmill, then flinches with pain and quickly starts again

> I think my point is clear.

As Aurora turns the treadmill, noxious fumes begin to pour out of some of the machinery

No. 24: Carabosse's Speech

> (*Singing*)And know, Aurora, as you work away,
> You're making smoke that will block out the day.
> I think that is a fitting retribution.
> (*To her acolytes*) Now we must go and stir up more pollution.
> (*Speaking*)And won't it be a comfort, as we make the world a mess
> To know Aurora's helping us to do it? Won't it?

Cinder } Yessss!
Smut

Cinder, Smut and Carabosse all hurry off, laughing wickedly

Aurora works away on her treadmill, looking pretty miserable

Florizel enters the auditorium holding the magic map in front of him. He is closely followed by Nurse Duneaux, the Marquis de Tarteauxpommes, and the two pages

Florizel We must be getting close. The light on the map's getting brighter.
Marquis (*pointing up towards the stage*) Look, your royal highness! There she is!
Florizel (*seeing Aurora and leaping up on to the stage*) Oh, my love, my love! What has happened to you?

Aurora stops walking to greet him, but winces with pain and starts again quickly

Act II, Scene 6

Aurora It's hopeless, Florizel. Carabosse has enchanted me. I am condemned to work forever on this treadmill.
Florizel I'll break in and set you free.
Aurora Impossible. The locks are magic. Only one spell can undo them.
Florizel Well, we must find that spell. (*To Nurse Duneaux, the Marquis de Tarteauxpommes and the pages*) Go on, start looking. See if there are any books of spells around the place.

The Marquis de Tarteauxpommes and the pages start looking around

Nurse (*to Florizel*) Aren't you forgetting something?
Florizel What?
Nurse The riddle. The riddle that Salamande gave you.
Florizel But I can't work it out. Listen.
      (*reading from the scroll*)
      "The power of good the power of bad defeats
      When all of these ingredients are blended —
      A pure heart, a kiss, what's in the seats,
      A stolen song — and evil will be ended!"
That could mean anything.
Marquis (*coming across the stage to listen*) Let's try and work it out, bit by bit. (*He looks over Florizel's shoulder at the scroll*) "A pure heart"…?
Nurse Well, that's certainly not me … (*He looks down into the audience*) as you'll find out later, (*man's name*). (*Turning back to Florizel*) But it could be Aurora … or you …
Marquis "A kiss"?
Nurse And I'm sure you and Aurora manage that between you.
Florizel } You bet!
Aurora }
Marquis "A stolen song"?
First Page (*finding a large scroll amidst the debris of the den*) I say, I've just found something funny over here.

The two pages carry the large scroll over to the Marquis

Nurse Duneaux What is it?
Marquis de Tarteauxpommes (*taking the scroll and opening it*) It would appear to be a poem about doing good to people.
Nurse Duneaux Don't sound like the sort of thing Carabosse would have.
Florizel No, it doesn't. (*He looks at the scroll*) No, it doesn't! (*With excitement*) And if it's not Carabosse's, what does that mean?
Marquis de Tarteauxpommes I've no idea.
Florizel It means that she's stolen it! And it's not a poem, it's a song! It's a stolen song!

Marquis de Tarteauxpommes Oh, terrific. So all we need is … (*he reads from the scroll*) … "what's in the seats"… Hm …
Florizel (*seeing the broken-down chairs*) Maybe there's some secret concealed inside these chairs.

While Aurora continues to work away on her treadmill, Florizel, the Marquis de Tarteauxpommes and the pages examine the chairs. Nurse Duneaux looks thoughtful, then looks out front, sees the audience and has an idea!

Nurse Duneaux (*pointing at the audience*) No, it's them!
Florizel What's them?
Nurse Duneaux They're "what's in the seats". The audience.
Florizel Of course!
Nurse Duneaux Come on, quickly, let's get this sorted out. You go and give Aurora a kiss. You bring that song over here, Tartie.
Marquis de Tarteauxpommes (*wincing*) Please don't call me Tartie.

Florizel goes to the cage where Aurora still pedals away

Florizel I'm afraid, Aurora, if you stop pedalling for a kiss, it may hurt you.
Aurora Don't worry. It'll be worth it!

Aurora stops pedalling, and faces Florizel. Through the bars of the cage, they manage quite a long kiss. Then, with a wince, Aurora breaks the contact and resumes pedalling

During this kiss, Nurse Duneaux teaches the audience the words of the song

Nurse Look, would you help us with this? Please. If we all sing the song together, and do the movements, I'm sure we can defeat Carabosse's magic. Come on, let's rehearse it through. Show them the words, Marquis.

The Marquis de Tarteauxpommes and Florizel hold the sides of the song sheet, while Nurse Duneaux leads the audience in singing

No. 25: The Power of Good

Nurse
We can break this spell
If we clap our hands,
And then stamp — one — two — three!
If we raise our swords
And shout:"Touché!",
The Power of Good we'll see!

Act II, Scene 6

Nurse Duneaux and the others take the audience through the words and movements of the song. Then they try to make the spell work. The first time nothing happens, so Nurse Duneaux exhorts the audience to greater volume. At the end of the second attempt, the treadmill stops, Aurora's chains come off her wrists and the doors of her cage spring open. She rushes into the arms of Florizel

Florizel Aurora!
Aurora Florizel! My hero!
Florizel We must escape! Come on, be quick!

Carabosse, with her acolytes in tow, appears in a puff of smoke

They try to bar the others' escape. Smut and Cinder are carrying chains and red-hot pincers, etc.

Carabosse Not quick enough. My little trick
Has worked so well, I have now in my caves,
Not one, but six weak and obedient slaves.
Marquis Incarcerate us, the men, by all means, but allow the women their freedom. (*He takes up a defensive posture in front of Nurse Duneaux*) I will not let you harm old Nurse Duneaux.
Nurse (*offended*) Less of the "old", you —
Carabosse No, none will I spare!
You all will feel my vengeance — so beware!
Cinder and Smut will add new pains to your distress.
Come, are you set to torture this lot?
Cinder }
Smut } (*brandishing their instruments of torture*) Yessss!

The acolytes advance to entrap the goodies. They capture and enchain Aurora, Nurse Duneaux, the two pages and the Marquis de Tarteauxpommes, but Florizel manages to wriggle free. He hurries across the room, and snatches up the pitchfork

Florizel To torture them, you'll have to kill me first!
Carabosse My pleasure, sonny. (*She snatches up a red-hot sword, and advances on Florizel*) Come on — do your worst!

To shouts of encouragement from the others, Carabosse and Florizel fight. Carabosse gains the upper hand, and forces him back until he is cornered against the furnace

Carabosse Now in my furnace burn, you little stinker!
And you'll come out a shapeless lump of clinker!

Florizel manages to push Carabosse sideways and get free, but he has lost his pitchfork in the process. Carabosse advances on him, swishing her sword with evil intent

Carabosse That's one escape. Don't think your life is charmed,
I have my sword still, and you are unarmed.

Carabosse continues her advance. Florizel trips on something, and lies on the stage at her mercy. She raises her sword for the coup de grâce. Nurse Duneaux suddenly has an idea and turns to the audience

Nurse Duneaux Once more! Just one more chorus of the song, and we might do it! It's worth trying. And louder than ever! One—two — three!!!

Carabosse turns in amazement to see what's happening. Nurse Duneaux and the Marquis de Tarteauxpommes, in spite of their chains, manage to hold out the words of the song

No. 25: The Power of Good

As soon as the song starts, the two acolytes look uneasy as if they're being crippled by something. Hissing, they pick up pitchforks and hold them up defensively, like shields. The effect on Carabosse is also dramatic. She staggers, apparently attacked by some internal pain. Unwillingly, with no control over her movements, she is dragged towards the mouth of the furnace

Nurse (*leading the audience in the song*)
We can break this spell
If we clap our hands,
And then stamp — one — two — three!
If we raise our swords and shout: 'Touché!',
The Power of Good we'll see!

As the song finishes, Carabosse disappears inside the furnace, to the sound of transformation music. There is an explosion and a puff of smoke

The exultant Florizel and Aurora fall into each other's arms. So, in the excitement of the moment, do Nurse Duneaux and the Marquis de Tarteauxpommes

The lighting changes to golden sunshine. Birdsong is heard, as shutters fall away from windows to reveal the palace gardens

Act II, Scene 6

The cast look around in amazement at the transformation

The King and Queen come rushing on and throw their arms around Aurora

King Aurora, my darling!
Queen I knew you'd be all right!

Salamande appears in a puff of smoke

Salamande From Kazakhstan my weary way I've wended,
Rejoicing that the evil reign is ended
Of Carabosse and every nasty minion ——
Nurse Hey, just a mo. Do you want my opinion?
Salamande What?
Nurse I think you try to do too much, Salamande. It's a common failing amongst do-gooders. You can't do everything for everyone. So my advice to you would be in future, concentrate on doing a few things well. If you'd been concentrating, and not gallivanting off round the world every couple of minutes, Aurora wouldn't have had half the trouble she has had.
Salamande Well ——
Nurse Sorry. Thought it needed saying.
Salamande Then thank you, Nurse. And while your words I'm
weighing.
I'll tell the rest of you about your future,
Make sure you all have tasks that suit yer.
You, King, will find, to match your own ability ——
King (*delightedly*) A quiet job with no responsibility!
Salamande And, Queen, when we have found a calling to
put him in ——
Queen I'll be campaigning to get votes for women!
Salamande Marquis, for you the future is, it seems,
Complete fulfilment of your——
Marquis Steamy dreams?

Salamande nods. The Marquis looks delighted

Salamande And for you, Nurse Duneaux, there's marriage in the air.
Nurse (*to the man in the front row of the audience*)
Well, goodness me. I thought we'd just have an affair.
Salamande And, Prince and Princess, what aims have you in sight?
Florizel To see the powers of science are used aright!
Aurora Yes, we've decided that, without apology,
We're going to learn to tame the new technology.

During these exchanges, Smut and Cinder have been trying to sidle off stage. But Salamande catches them by the ears

No. 26: Salamande's Speech
Salamande (*singing*)And you will come along with me, you two,
'Cos I've got lots of work for you to do.

Cinder and Smut grimace at the prospect. Salamande addresses the assembled cast

> Tomorrow, friends, I'm glad to tell,
> Is the day Aurora weds her Florizel.
> Their joy will grow — it cannot be diminish'd
> The reign of Carabosse is —
> (*Speaking*) finished!

All Hooray!

Everyone hurries off stage

Nurse Duneaux, Marquis de Tarteauxpommes and the two Pages remain on stage. Nurse Duneaux starts spinning the pages round and looking at them intently

Marquis What are you doing?
Nurse Reading.
Marquis de Tarteauxpommes What are you reading?
Nurse I don't know — but it's a real page turner! (*She roars with laughter*)

The two pages run off stage, giggling

(*Eyeing up the Marquis rather beadily*) You know, I couldn't help noticing, Tartie, when old Carabosse was threatening me, you stood up to her ——
Marquis (*flustered*) It was no more than any other correctly brought-up gentleman would have done in the circumstances.
Nurse Ooh, I think it was.
Marquis (*with a degree of dread*) Oh.
Nurse I'm afraid the truth of the matter is... however much we fudge around it, Tartie... you and I were made for each other.
Marquis Oh dear.

The Marquis and Nurse Duneaux sing a short reprise

No. 27: If I Ever End Up With You (Reprise)
Nurse You are chalk and I am cheese, but we are a team.
Marquis (*coming round*) Just like coffee and cream.

Act II, Scene 6

Nurse	Let's get married then.
Marquis	We'll work up a steam.
Nurse	(*with a wink to the audience, speaking*) Get stoking.
Both	(*singing*) If I ever end up with you…
Marquis	(*uncertain*) Would a woman let me be master?
Nurse	(*urging him on*) Well, you'll never know till you've ask'd her,
	Go on, have a go!
Marquis	(*speaking*) Oh, I really don't know.
Nurse	(*singing*) If I ever end up with you,
	Well, it wouldn't be such a disaster.
	We could find some continuity
	As a twosome.
Marquis	And the thought of perpetuity's
	Not so gruesome.
Nurse	(*speaking*) We could share our mirth and merriment!
Marquis	(*speaking*) You could help me to experiment!
Nurse	(*speaking*) Yes, I've sure got that ability!
Marquis	(*speaking*) So we've found compatability!
Nurse	(*speaking*) We'll grow old and and watch the scenery!
Marquis	(*speaking*) Look ahead to our centenary!
Both	(*looking at each other soupily*) Aaaah! …
	(*singing*) If I ever end up with you.

Nurse (*speaking*) Put it there.

They end up in a dewy-eyed clinch and kiss

  Right you are then. Tomorrow's going to a double wedding.
Marquis Is it? Oh, gosh.
Nurse Now you just run along, will you, Tartie? I've got something to do.
Marquis And what might that be?
Nurse Don't ask. If you and I are going to stay married, we have to have a few secrets from each other.
Marquis (*as he goes off*) Oh, very well. I'm sure you know best.

The Marquis de Tarteauxpommes exits

Nurse (*to the audience, after the Marquis has gone*) "I'm sure you know best" — that was good. He's sounding like a husband already, isn't he? I'll just have to stop him using all those long words, and he'll start to be quite human. (*She hurries down to the front of the stage and looks at the man she's targeted in the audience*) I'm sorry about this. But see — he's got a title. You haven't got a title, have you? No, thought not. So I'm sorry ... Today ... Dressing room after the show ... (*she shakes her head ruefully*) ... better not. (*She makes her way to an exit and stops just before going off*) In a couple of years, though, (*man's name*)— who knows? Give me a call.

Nurse Duneaux exits

No. 28: Finale

A fanfare sounds

   Salamande, Cinder and Smut and the pages enter, carrying luggage

The company sings the wedding day finale

All
   Welcome This Glorious day (Reprise)
Welcome this glorious day
With joy, 'cause we're happy to say
The King and the Queen's very beautiful child
Is marrying her fiancé.

At this point a steam train puffs on stage, proudly driven by the Marquis de Tarteauxpommes, with the King as guard, and containing Florizel and Aurora

The Marquis steps out and sings

Marquis
   Steamy Dreams (Reprise)
Here it is, that dream again,
As I lie in my bed...
Steamy dreams — driving me insane —
Ready — steady — steam ahead!

Steam — steam — funny, but it always seems
Steam trains rattle thro' my steamy dreams!

   The King and Queen enter

Florizel and Aurora step out of the train and sing

Florizel
   Awakenings(Reprise)
I am a prince, I've loved you since
The moment I first saw you.

Act II, Scene 6

Aurora I feel so sure we've met before,
I know I will adore you.
Both And so always, through all my days,
I'll live my whole life for you.
I'll live it all for…
I'll live it all for you.

Nurse Duneaux hurries on stage, dressed for travel

Welcome This Glorious Day (Reprise)
All Princess Aurora has got the lot,
Riches you cannot compare.
And to completely round off the plot
Now she's got someone to share.
We wish her and her Florizel
Freedom from worry and care!

Sound out a hip-hip-hooray
And chase all your sadness away
For Princess Aurora, the beautiful child,
Is going to be married today.
Is going to be married today!
Today, Hooray!

The cast wave to the audience. The train moves off

The cast sing the following reprises whilst they go into their curtain call routine

No. 29: Curtain Calls

Get Up To Date
You've got so much on your plate
You can't stay and vegetate
The past is gone, the future's great
What you've got to do is
Get up to date
Get up to date
Up to date
All you got to do is get up to date

Welcome This Glorious Day
Sound out a hip hip hooray

And chase all your sadness away
For Princess Aurora, the beautiful child
Is going to be married today
Today,
Hooray

The Curtain *falls*

FURNITURE AND PROPERTY LIST

ACT I

Scene 1

On stage: The palace throne room
The two royal thrones

Off stage: Baby Princess Aurora, robed in a christening gown

Personal: **Salamande:** magic wand
Carabosse: magic wand

Scene 2

On stage: New forest cloth

Scene 3

On stage: Eighteenth-century garden furniture for the palace garden
Two shepherd's crooks for **Queen Georgette** and **Aurora**

Off stage: Time machine (see page 11-12 for description)

Personal: **Marquis de Tarteauxpommes:** bunch of keys

Scene 4

On stage: Palace corridor cloth

Off stage: Golden bag of sweets
Bunch of keys (**Nurse Duneaux**)
Two trays with large, wobbly, pink jellies
Tray with two cream cakes
Tray with large cake decorated with whipped cream
A small barrel containing wine
Three silver wine jugs; one containing confetti or shredded paper
Large french loaf about five feet long

Furniture and Property List

Scene 5

On stage: Secret room in tower dating from an earlier period than the rest of the tower
Dust and cobwebs over room and furniture
Spinning wheel
Stool

Personal: **Nurse Duneaux**: bunch of keys

Scene 6

On stage: Palace corridor cloth

Scene 7

On stage: Throne room as Scene 1
Golden bier for **Aurora**

Off stage: Black mourning sashes
White flowers
Golden bag of sweets for **King Pantalouse**

ACT II

Scene 1

On stage: Overgrown forest cloth

Off stage: Map for **Florizel**
Shooting stick for **Marquis de Tarteauxpommes**
Two lanterns

Personal: **Carabosse**: long dagger

Scene 2

On stage: Throne room as Act I Scene 7
Dust and cobwebs on furniture and cast

Off stage: Large old-fashioned camera on a tripod

Scene 3

On stage: Overgrown forest cloth

Scene 4

On stage: Palace throne room as ACT I SCENE 1
Time machine

Off stage: Trumpet for **Queen Georgette**
Small scroll for **Salamande**
Magic map for **Salamande**

Scene 5

On stage: Overgrown forest cloth

Scene 6

On stage: **Carabosse**'s den
Various machines and broken-down chairs
Metal cage containing an old treadmill
Fiery furnace with various red-hot swords inside
Pitch fork
Large scroll with words of song **No.25 The Power of Good**

Off stage: Magic map
Scroll
Chains and red hot-pincers etc.
Luggage
Steam train

LIGHTING PLOT

Practical fittings required: magnesium flash for camera, glowing mouth of a furnace

ACT I

Scene 1

To open: Overall general lighting

No cues

Scene 2

To open: Overall general lighting

No cues

Scene 3

To open: Overall general lighting

No cues

Scene 4

To open: Overall general lighting

No cues

Scene 5

To open: Semi-darkness

Cue 1 **Carabosse** sings the "Spinning Song" (Page 24)
Light slowly builds throughout song, but only to a point that remains murky and threatening

Cue 2 **Aurora**'s hand is impaled on the spindle (Page 25)
Flash of red light

Scene 6

To open: Overall general lighting

No cues

Scene 7

To open: Overall general lighting

No cues

ACT II

Scene 1

To open: Overall general lighting

No cues

Scene 2

To open: Semi-darkness

Cue 3   **Florizel** and the **Marquis de Tarteauxpommes** enter   (Page 37)
The lanterns spread more light, which continues to build as the scene progresses

Cue 4   **Florizel** looks around the throne room in bewilderment   (Page 38)
*Shaft of light on **Aurora**'s bier*

Cue 5   The cast hold a pose for the camera   (Page 43)
Magnesium flashes and the lights fade

Scene 3

To open: Overall general lighting

No cues

Scene 4

To open: Overall general lighting

No cues

Lighting Plot

Scene 5

To open: Overall general lighting

Cue 6 **Florizel** enters through the auditorium (Page 50)
Bring up house lights or follow spots

Scene 6

To open: Lighting to suggest the noxious sink of nineteenth century industrial waste. Glowing mouth of a fiery furnace

Cue 7 **Nurse** and the **Marquis** fall into each other's arms (Page 58)
Lighting changes to golden sunshine

EFFECTS PLOT

ACT I

Cue 1	**Marquis**: "... you ill-mannered ——" *Puff of smoke*	(Page 4)
Cue 2	**Salamande:** "... joy and love." *Puff of smoke on opposite side of the stage*	(Page 4)
Cue 3	**Carabosse**: "... curse of Carabosse." *Puff of smoke*	(Page 6)
Cue 4	**Salamande**: "...'Come back, Salamande!'" *Puff of smoke*	(Page 7)
Cue 5	**The Marquis** throws a switch *The time machine starts to hiss and steam puffs out the top*	(Page 12)
Cue 6	**The Marquis** fiddles with the controls of the time machine *Bubbling and hissing noises begin to build up*	(Page 13)
Cue 7	**Aurora:** "... exciting!" *The noises of hissing and bubbling increase*	(Page 13)
Cue 8	The time machine starts to shake from side to side *More steam comes puffing out of various crevices. Finally there is the sound of an explosion*	(Page 13)
Cue 9	**Nurse Duneaux and the Marquis**: "... with you." *Explosion from inside the time machine. Smoke puffs out and hissing sounds*	(Page 17)
Cue 10	**Nurse Duneaux**: " ... work to be done." *Clattering of crockery and cutlery offstage*	(Page 18)
Cue 11	**Nurse Duneaux**: " ... need filling!" *More clattering is heard offstage*	(Page 19)
Cue 12	**Nurse Duneaux** chases a scullion off stage *Loud crash as if someone's run into a pile of metal dishes*	(Page 19)

Effects Plot

Cue 13	The two scullions exit either side of the stage *Clanging and clattering offstage*	(Page 20)
Cue 14	**Carabosse:** " ... Spinning thro' the night." *Sound of key turning in a heavy lock*	(Page 24)
Cue 15	**All cast and Audience**: "Come back, Salamande!" *Puff of smoke*	(Page 29)

ACT II

Cue 16	To open *Puff of smoke*	(Page 33)
Cue 17	**Florizel** and the **Marquis** set off into the forest *Spooky music sounds*	(Page 37)
Cue 18	To open Scene 3 *Puff of smoke*	(Page 44)
Cue 19	**Aurora**: "Yes." *Steam starts to puff out from the time machine*	(Page 45)
Cue 20	**The Marquis** pulls presses a switch on the time machine *Smoke pours out and bubbling noises come out* *of the time machine*	(Page 46)
Cue 21	**Carabosse** pulls the curtain of the time machine across *The machine makes bubbling noises and steam puffs out* *of it*	(Page 47)
Cue 22	**Queen Georgette**: "... Come back, Salamande!" *Puff of smoke*	(Page 48)
Cue 23	To open Scene 6 *Smoke, clouds of "poisonous" vapours,* *sounds of unnamed machines chug and clunk*	(Page 52)
Cue 24	**Aurora** starts to work the treadmill *sound of mechanical clunking*	(Page 53)
Cue 25	**Aurora** stops on the treadmill *Sound of mechanical clunking stops*	(Page 54)
Cue 26	**Aurora** turns the treadmill *"Noxious" fumes pour out of the machinery*	(Page 54)

Cue 27	**Florizel**: "... be quick!" *Puff of smoke*	(Page 57)
Cue 28	**Carabosse** disappears inside the furnace *Transformation music sounds, followed by an explosion and a puff of smoke*	(Page 58)
Cue 29	The **Nurse** and the **Marquis** fall into each other's arms *Birdsong sounds*	(Page 58)
Cue 30	**Queen**: "... all right!" *Puff of smoke*	(Page 59)
Cue 31	**All**: "...is marrying her fiancé" *Sounds of steam train entering, steam*	(Page 62)

www.ingramcontent.com/pod-product-compliance
Ingram Content Group UK Ltd.
Pitfield, Milton Keynes, MK11 3LW, UK
UKHW021845210426
5322IPUK00022B/476